THE MULTIHANDICAPPED: SERVING THE SEVERELY DISABLED

by

Jack M. Gootzeit, Ed.D.

with
Contributions by

Betty Meyer, M.S.

* Illustrator: Betty Meyer *

✳IRVINGTON PUBLISHERS, Inc., New York

RM
930
G66
1981

Library of Congress Cataloging in Publication Data

ISBN 0-8290-0556-0

BT 11,269-82   6/18/82

Printed in the United States of America

CONTENTS

LIST OF ILLUSTRATIONS.. x

FOREWORD: L.A. EVANGELISTA, M.D... xi

PREFACE: NOTE FROM HOWARD A. NEWBURGER, Ph.D..................... xii

AUTHOR'S NOTE xiii

I   INTRODUCTION 1

II   THE SEVERELY AND PROFOUNDLY HANDICAPPED. 4

III DISABILITY 8
Some Functions That Are Manifested by a Lack or Loss of Ability 8
   Retardation.. 8
   Cerebral Palsy and Later Motor Impairment.. 9
   Autism... 10
   Emotional Disturbance 11
   Other Inabilities 11
Developmental Disabilities 12
   Innate Releasor Mechanisms (IRM's) 12
   IRM's and Development 13
   IRM's: Use and Disuse in the Evolution of Ability and Disability.... 13
      At the Cellular Level.. 14
      At the Level of Circulation 14
      Respiration 15
       Using IRM's to Induce Normative Breathing in the Cerebral Palsied .. 15
      Bone 16
      Joints... 17
      Nerve 17
      Muscle... 17
Constancy and Constant Environmental Conditions 17
In Conclusion 17

IV   PRINCIPLES FOR HABILITATION, EDUCATION, AND
     RECREATION FOR THE SEVERELY AND PROFOUNDLY
     HANDICAPPED. THE TIME AND PLACE FOR PROGRAM 19
Staff and Workers 20
The Time for the Programs 22
The Principles of the Program 22

V   THE DEVELOPMENT OF ACTIVITY
     OF THE NERVOUS SYSTEM.. 24
The Sensory System.. 26
Development of Behavior.. 28
Defects in Development 30
Homeostasis and Activity.. 30
Fatigue 32
The Genesis of Activity... 33
Postnatal Development of Cerebral Activity... 35

The Nerve... 36
Action Potential 37
The Integration of Nervous Activity.. 38
Inhibition and Habituation 40
Mind and Electrical Brain Factors 41
Message Theory... 42
Feedback 42
Learning 43
Memory 44
Cortical Tonicity and Integration 44
Brain Wave Variations 46
Consciousness.. 46
Conclusion 47

VI   THE BASIC RECEIVING SYSTEMS AND THE MODALITIES
      OF RESPONSE (With Maryann P. Toomey, M.S.) 50
Perception.. 51
Basic Orientation 51
Auditory 52
Visual 54
Olfactory (Odor-Nose) 55
Gustatory (Eating System) 55
Thermal.. 56
Pressure/Pain 56
The Haptic Sense.. 57
Proprioception... 57
Spatial Discrimination 57
The Motor Area.. 58

VII   THE GOOTZEIT PROCEDURE TO DETERMINE WHETHER
      OR NOT TO USE TRADITIONAL OR REFLEXIVE
      EXERCISE PROCEDURES.. 60
Neck Extension 60
The Abdominals 64
Hip Extension and Flexion.. 66
Creeping 67
Crawling 69
Standing... 70
Walking.. 73
Hands, Arms, and Forearms 74
Grasp 75

VIII THE HIGHER MENTAL PROCESSES 77
Exploration.. 77
The Neural Behavior Net (NBN)... 77
Rehearsal and Recall.. 79
Comprehension 79
Problem-Solving Activity... 79

Cognition 79
Learning and Perception 79
Behavior and Its Development 80
IX   EFFECTING COMMUNICATION AND INTERACTION 82
Awareness, Focus, and Attention 82
    Awareness 82
        Seizures: The Gootzeit Maneuver for Treatment 84
    Focus 85
    Attention and Habituation 86
X   BEHAVIOR MODIFICATION (With Rose Marie Hughes) 87
Systems of Behavior Modification 87
The Gootzeit System:
An Adaptation from a Neo-Hullian Concept of Behavior 88
    Unlearned Reflex Connections 88
    Needs and Neural Behavior Nets 90
    Drive States 90
    Conditioned Stimulus 91
    Reinforcement and Operant Conditioning 93
    Habituation 93
Gootzeit Behavioral Modification Techniques 94
    Acting-Up Individuals 96
    Specific Gootzeit Techniques for Controlling an Acting-Up Individual 98
XI   EFFECTING PURPOSIVE ACTIVITY 105
Effecting Object Relations 106
Eliciting of Color Relations 107
Rationale for a Directive Method 108
XII THERAPEUTIC RECREATION AND ACTIVITY 112
Recreation as a Developmental Concept 112
Therapy and Recreation 113
The Severely Involved and Profoundly Retarded 113
The Rehabilitative Process 116
Segregation Versus Integration 116
XIII THE NEED FOR PERSONAL ADJUSTMENT TRAINING.
     A SYSTEM OF BEHAVIOR MODIFICATION 118
Foundations for P.A.T.: A Review of Research 118
The Need for P.A.T.: A Review of Research 120
    Adjustment Training and the World of Work 120
    Adjusting to the Work World: A Developmental View 122
    Adjustment to Work: Importance of Physical Factors 123
    Work Adjustment and the Home Environment 123
    Parental Attitudes 124
An Example of a P.A.T. Program 125
    General Concepts 125
    The A.R.C. Program 126

The Diagnostic Use of Personal Adjustment Training
in Work Activity Centers.. 127
A Broad Proposal for a P.A.T. Program.. 129
XIV PROGRAMMING OF THE MULTIHANDICAPPED
       IN A WORK ACTIVITY CENTER (James Meyer, B.A.)...................... 132
XV A HANDBOOK FOR PERSONAL ADJUSTMENT TRAINING........ 137
Chapter One. Introduction 139
   Goals of Training 141
   Methods of Training 143
   Objectives of P.A.T.. 143
   Definition of Personal Adjustment Training (P.A.T.) 144
   The World of Work and P.A.T... 144
   Scope and Depth of the Handbook.. 145
   "Division of Labor" Within P.A.T. 147
Chapter Two. Physical Adjustment to Work 148
   Coordination.. 148
      Assessing Problems of Coordination.. 148
      Methods of Modifying Coordination Problems 148
   The Senses 149
   Ability to Talk.. 149
   Physical Demands of Work 149
   Physical Skills 150
   Work Judgment 150
   Work Pace 150
   Fatigue.. 151
   Work Tolerance and Flexibility... 151
Chapter Three. Work Habits and Adjustment to Work...................... 153
   Definition of Work Habits.. 153
   Attention to Duties, Attention Span, and Concentration on Work 153
   Consistency and the Repetitive Nature of Work............................ 154
   Regular Hours of Work 154
   Routine Motor Habits 155
   Specific Work Space for Each Worker 155
   Travel 155
   Wages and Pay.. 156
   Safety.. 156
      Smoking Habits 157
   Jobs Available to the Multi-Handicapped 157
   Work Interruptions.. 158
   Work Attitudes.. 159
   Concepts the Client Must Understand.. 159
   Personal Habits Related to Work Adjustment 160
   Positive Disapprobation (Punishment)... 160
Chapter Four. Personal and Interpersonal Factors
and Concepts Related to Work 161

Working with Others and Dealing with People..161
Ability to Face Impersonal Relations and to be Impersonal 161
Ability to Meet and Deal with the Public 162
Competition 162
    Reaction to Authority...162
    Handling Authority..162
    Facing Employers and Dependence on Authority.....................................163
    Rejection by Authority 163
Developing Work Ability in the Handicapped...164
Satisfactions..165
Religions, Race and Culture: Contact and Ethnic Differences 165
The Way Others View the Client 166
Acceptance of a Client on a Job...167
Meeting the Client's Needs...168
Special Problems 168
    Persistence of a Problem...168
    The "Detached Client" 169
    Other Maladaptive Behavior...169
Chapter Five. Competencies and Techniques Needed
by Members of a P.A.T. Staff..171
The Need for Special Competencies in P.A.T Personnel 171
Roles and Status in a P.A.T. Setting 172
    The Professional...172
    The Nonprofessional 173
Summary of Competencies Needed by P.A.T. Professionals.........................173
    General 173
    Specialized 174
In Conclusion 175

APPENDICES 177
A.   EXCERPTS FROM PARENTS' LETTERS..179
B.   PROCEDURES FOR TESTING MOTOR FUNCTIONING
       AND REFLEXES (With Rose Marie Hughes) 183
C.   FUNCTIONAL CATEGORIES OF MULTIHANDICAPPED 194

BIBLIOGRAPHY..204
INDEX...207

LIST OF ILLUSTRATIONS

Figure   Page

1. NECK EXTENSION. Gootzeit Procedure One 61
2. NECK EXTENSION. Gootzeit Procedure Two 62
3. NECK EXTENSION. Gootzeit Procedure Three 63
4. THE ABDOMINALS. Gootzeit Procedure One 64
5. THE ABDOMINALS. Gootzeit Procedure Two 65
6. HIP EXTENSION—HIP FLEXION. Gootzeit Procedures
   One and Two 66
7. CREEPING. Gootzeit Procedure, Step One 67
8. CREEPING. Gootzeit Procedure, Step Two 68
9. CREEPING. Gootzeit Procedure, Step Three 68
10. CRAWLING. Gootzeit Procedure One (a, b) 69
    CRAWLING. Gootzeit Procedure Two (c) 70
11. STANDING. Gootzeit Procedure One 70
12. STANDING. Gootzeit Procedure Two 71
13. STANDING. Gootzeit Procedure Three 72
14. WALKING. Gootzeit Procedure One 73
15. WALKING. Gootzeit Procedure Two 74
16. STRENGTHENING HANDS, ARMS, AND FOREARMS.
    Wrist and Hand Supination 75
17. GOOTZEIT TECHNIQUES FOR CONTROLLING ACTING-UP
    INDIVIDUALS. Procedure One (Cross-Chest) 98
18. GOOTZEIT TECHNIQUES, (etc.). Procedure Two 99
19. GOOTZEIT TECHNIQUES, (etc.). Procedure Three 100
20. GOOTZEIT TECHNIQUES, (etc.). Procedure Four 100
21. GOOTZEIT TECHNIQUES, (etc.). Procedure Five 101
22. GOOTZEIT TECHNIQUES, (etc.). Procedure Six 102
23. GOOTZEIT TECHNIQUES, (etc.). Procedure Seven
    (Long Control Method) 102
24. GOOTZEIT TECHNIQUES, (etc.). Procedure Eight
    (Block and Parry) 103

Table   Page

1. A CLASSICAL CONDITIONING PROCESS 92

FOREWORD

The work of Jack M. Gootzeit, Ed.D., should be of interest to professionals in a number of fields, including medicine, physical and occupational therapy, educational psychology, special education, and other disciplines concerned with habilitation.

His book is based on twenty-seven years of experience in the clinical applied art and science of treatment and education of hundreds of the severely or profoundly multihandicapped—infants, children, and adults—at the Institutes of Applied Human Dynamics in New York City and St. Jude's Habilitation Institute in Valhalla, New York.

Dr. Gootzeit is a rehabilitation generalist. He is a licensed physical therapist, a certified school psychologist, a rehabilitation counselor; he also has a masters degree in therapeutic recreation. Over the years he has served as Adjunct Associate Professor of Physical Education at Hunter College, teaching movement behavior; and as Adjunct Associate Professor of Education at Pace University, Westchester, New York.

This book is the outgrowth of many seminars and lectures and it reflects Dr. Gootzeit's multidisciplinary background. His broad experience and useful practical suggestions should assist practitioners in many fields who work with severely and profoundly multihandicapped individuals of all ages.

Lilia A. Evangelista, M.D.
(Consultant, Clinical Services, IAHD)
Medical Director,
Children's Evaluation and Rehabilitation Clinic
Lincoln Hospital

PREFACE

These papers by Dr. Jack M. Gootzeit are the essence of the continuing seminars held by the Institutes of Applied Human Dynamics over the last twenty-seven years.

The theories presented in this publication add neuro-physiological and reflex dynamics to the day-to-day tools of the educator, recreationist, child development worker and all those concerned with normally developing children as well as the handicapped.

Individuals interested in the techniques now so successfully employed at the Institutes will find that these writings and lectures, together with Dr. Gootzeit's already published works, represent the theoretical and philosophical framework of the Institutes.

Howard A. Newburger, Ph.D.
(Director of Faculty, IAHD)
Formerly Professor and Department Chairman,
New York University

AUTHOR'S NOTE

The author wishes to thank Maureen Vincie for her expert help in the writing and editing of this book; and Maryanne P. Toomey, M.S. and Rose Marie Hughes for their special contributions in Chapter VI and Appendix C, respectively.

Most specially, my thanks always to the children, adults, parents, and staff of the Institutes, who have made all the years worthwhile.

—Jack M. Gootzeit

CHAPTER I

Introduction

Laboratory techniques are the most appropriate techniques for scientific studies: subjects can be selected by sex and heredity; they can be observed for twenty-four hour periods; and prior conditions and factors can be recorded. However, we are interested in modifying behavior in life situations. Here prior conditions, heredities, and behaviors are observed during limited time surveys (hours, days, etc.) and not in relation to all conditions, Therefore, the techniques we employ are clinical—the application of helping arts and scientific techniques and information to the on-going and applied situations of everyday life. The effects of diet, heredity, prior conditions and life situations will bring fluctuation and change from day to day, hour to hour, and minute to minute. Thus an applied science implies that scientific information and technique must be elaborated and implemented in the present, by persons who can utilize such information in each unique situation—and individualize and apply those techniques to each person.

The entire mechanism of voluntary movement and mental activity is a conditioned-associated process, If we have a series of positive (as well as inhibitory) reflexes from stimuli of different intensities and apply them for some time—day to day, with definite and equal intervals between stimuli, and always in the same order—we establish in the cortex a stereotype of processes. If we repeat one of the stimuli it then produces the same order of response.

We enhance the frequency of response, or inhibition, to a given stimulus by (a) eliciting the response repetitively, whereby each occurence tends to favor a particular response to a particular stimulus (Law of Exercise); and by (b) operantly reinforcing positively (rewarding) or aversively conditioning (punishing) the response. Positive reinforcement tends to increase the frequency of a response. Aversive conditioning tends to cause an inhibition or decrement in frequency of response.

Thus, we bracket a behavior by a classic conditioning stimulus, one which forces each action to happen. We increase the frequency of a response and strengthen the response by its repetition under given stimulus conditions. Then we operantly positively reinforce or aversively condition, in relation to a situation, to increase or decrease the frequency of response.

These behavior modification techniques are the foundation of both our motor and intellectual behavior development programs. They are applicable to the entire range of developmental problems involving the severely neurologically impaired, the hyperactive, and the emotionally disturbed.

The above hypotheses, together with the gathering of evidence and clinical experience, represent the basis upon which rests our concept of the physiology, sociology, and psychology of how behavior develops, is reinforced, and becomes strengthened by use. This is fundamental to our concept of the effect of *use* (as well as *disuse*).

There is a physics, chemistry, biology, physiology, psychology, and sociology of use and disuse. Life, as Theilard deChardin writes, is a continuous process of evolving from active fields of interaction between crystalline substances to the evolving complexity of living cells to the processes we call awareness and intelligence.

Processes related to disuse are viewed conceptually as in an inert state. That is to say, they are in a condition where all change is at a standstill, a state in which all physical, psychological, and chemical activity ceases.

"Use" is made (a change in activity state), when substances are changed from one physical state to another (liquid, gas, crystalline). These substances are twisted, stretched, or displaced; or pass into elecrical, ionic, or magnetic fields, or are influenced by them. This results in a change in the electric, thermodynamic, piezoelectric, thermoelectric, pryoelectric, humor-chemical, and neurochemical qualities of these substances and their energy relationships. These changes, in turn, affect the chemistry, physiology, psychology, etc., of yet other substances, particularly in living systems and the workings of these systems that will affect behavior.

A review of the literature implies that much of the prenatal development of a fetus is related to its level of stimulation. The ascending (sensory) pathways develop first. Then, as stimuli impinge on the action mechanism of the brain, processes grow structurally to integrate the lower centers of behavior (the medulla, spinal cord, myoneural fibers, etc.). In addition, use and disuse of neural pathways affect the volume of neuroplasm—which seems also to be correlated with the electrical activity of the brain. This electrical activity can be demonstrated on the electroencephalograph. The volumes of neuroplasm can be demonstrated by comparing neural material microscopically before and after periods of activity.

Prenatal conditions are not subject to intervention by the educator or clinician. However, physical activity programs and clinical electrical stimulation techniques may have a direct relationship to the postnatal development of reflexes and activity. Both muscle and higher process cortical activity seem to grow in relation to levels of stimulation. From massive random and incoordinate reactions, specific and refined actions are seen to emerge even in a structural sense. Current scientific data make it plausable that at certain levels of development, massive, repeated, and intensive stimulation can accelerate and elaborate the development of cortical centers. As educators, experimental techniques for eliciting physical development are important to our work with the neurologically impaired and should be integrated into our teaching and training programs.

Thus, activity is our continual pursuit at the Institutes of Applied Human Dynamics, as it is activity that effects changes in the physiological, social, and mental processes that have come to be known as intelligence.

CHAPTER II

The Severely And
Profoundly Handicapped

The severely and profoundly handicapped are a comglomerate of disability conditions. They are typically and often systematically excluded from the treatment and rehabilitation community of services.

The conditions that compose the entity we call the severely and profoundly handicapped are merely extreme examples of disabilities that have in the past thirty-five to fifty years become the trade subjects for rehabilitation services: cerebral palsy, autism, retardation, schizophrenia, the sensory disabilities (blindness, auditory impairment), the perceptually handicapped, and the learning disabled.

The following are some common indicators that preclude membership in a given disability entity (i.e., political/agency entity) such as cerebral palsy, autism, or retardation:

1. If "improveability" is not prognosticated or if it is so slow as to lose the interest of the physician, therapist, or treatment facility.

2. Mixtures of disabilities. These "permit" the disability agency to disavow responsibility.

3. Professional decisions to handle a condition custodially rather than by an active program of treatment, rehabilitation, and education. These decisions are aften based on economic conditions rather than clinical feasibility.

Furthermore, there are other intensely handicapping symptoms which often cause exclusion from a treatable disability entity:

1. Lack of initial progress.

2. Contractures; bone and joint deformities.

3. Severe ataxia (loss or lack of balance).

4. Severe spasticity.

5. Severe hyperactivity and "acting up."

6. Loss or lack of hearing, visual, or verbal communication.

7. Random wandering and lack of apparent contact.

8. Lack of demonstrated relations to persons or objects.

9. Severe problems in eating and/or toileting.

10. Frequent or uncontrolled behavior disorders.
11. I.Q. below 33.
12. Aging—particularly as it affects growth and size, and the
    number of helpers needed to feed, care for, and handle the
    needs of an individual.

Many persons may be differentially categorized as severely handicapped at anytime during their lives, particularly after initial attempts at
correction. For the developmentally disabled (as they grow older), more
and more of those who fail to respond (improve) are put into the category
of the severely disabled.

Until recently, when a person was categorized as severely or profoundly
handicapped, there was an accompanying intention to place that individual in a custodial category. This is a designation that elicits little human
concern and allows only for such basic life services as toileting, feeding,
nursing, and domiciliary care.

For example, an eighty-five-year-old gentleman who had a heart condition also suffered a right, below-knee amputation as a sequella of diabetes.
He was denied a leg prosthesis because "it would be a waste of funds."
However, the physical therapists at a local department of physical
medicine rejected this decision. They decided to make a plaster pilon and
peg leg, and it was utilized to bring this man back to a level of independent
ambulation. Only as a result of these efforts was agreement with the
funding agency achieved, and the gentleman was fitted with a prosthesis.

Other persons who often swell the ranks of the severely and profoundly
handicapped are the autistic, schizophrenic, hyperactive and learning
disabled—persons who, after passing the age of improveability (seven to
twelve) are dropped from community service and education programs or
pressed into institutions. We feel that such decisions are made not on the
grounds of intellectual ability or disability but because these people could
not be serviced by the treatment facilities. These facilities have traditionally assumed that such children become disorganized in their adolescence and hence they abandon them.

The result of this abandonment is that these children either sit home
without service or are put by the hundreds into custodial institutions.
Here they regress socially, intellectually, and emotionally, often losing
even self-care skills such as self-feeding, toileting, and elementary grooming. Many of these children, because of their random or bizarre behavior
and hyperactivity, have been placed in locked infirmaries with impersonal
attendants. Many are tied into bed or prevented from moving by restrictive devices. It is no wonder that so many have become even more disturbed, more retarded, and more regressed, incontinent, and fearsome.
Having thus reached this condition, these children fulfilled the prediction
that they were unimproveable.

Yet, in working with hundreds of severely and profoundly handicapped persons over the past twenty-five years, we have found that each handicapped person can progress, improve, and benefit from an active intervening education, rehabilitation, and therapeutic recreation program. Work with the severely and profoundly handicapped *always* results in some improvement. Often it results in profound improvement. Disabilities once very severe are modified. Every once in a while a person moves to a higher functioning level: sometimes to a borderline level and, on a rare occasion, to near normalcy. In some cases the individual passes out of the population of the recognized handicap and integrates fully into the general population.

Thus, because their combination of disabilities and/or the severity of their disabilities have excluded them from services offered by agencies serving specific disabilities and, because of our years of experience, we prefer to categorize our clients as the severely and profoundly handicapped-still better, the multihandicapped.

Many of the agencies who serve moderately or mildly handicapped individuals have supported a type of nonapproach to certain clients, one in which persons are labeled with the terms "severe" and "profound." Indeed, the most widely used label for evading further responsibiity for a treatment plan is that of "severely or profoundly retarded." In this manner the vicious circle of custodial care and regression is initiated, and the self-fulfilling prophecies of the institutionalization approach are once more corroborated. A downward spiral is begun, and unending bedcare, disuse (and resulting neurological disability), loss of mental ability, withdrawal from environmental contact (for self-protection from hostility), and a lack of focus and attention to childhood needs are the consequences of this traditional approach. The client becomes locked into a "catch-22" situation: institutionalization results in inactivity, and inactivity brings further disability from disuse. This increased helplessness leads to further and more severe disabilities—all of which leads to a still further diminution of treatment of services.

The American Association for Mental Deficiency's definition of Mental Retardation is considered the most broadly accepted concept of that disability: Mental retardation is a mental subnormality indicated in infancy and attaining in adulthood. Why then do so many physicians diagnose a child as severely or profoundly retarded —long before outcomes are functionally tested and long before the child has attained childhood?

The consequence of such an early diagnosis results in children being denied basic corrective services which, in themselves, might affect a child's basic intellectual functioning. For example:

—Gail, a young retarded woman of 18, was observed to be squinting and holding pictures very close to her eyes. She was sent for an eye examination by an O.V.R. Counselor. The physician did a refraction and found that Gail had a correctable problem. But he did not recommend glasses because she had an I.Q. of only 45.

—Walter, a hyperactive fifteen-year-old, had a severe hearing deficiency and was found to be legally blind. He was denied a hearing aid and glasses because "he would be too retarded to benefit from them."

And yet, the sensory modalities themselves are contributory components of mental retardation. The correction of any deficiencies could have a profound effect on improveability.

A similar situation involved a group of children at a physical rehabilitation center in Westchester. These children were severely spastic and failed to show initial improveability while at the center. They were then labeled "profoundly retarded."

—Gina, one of these children, was later taught to walk with assistance at our facility. Prior to this, a referral was made to the Westchester center to obtain leg braces to prevent a possible deformity at the ankle. Gina was denied the brace because "she was too retarded to understand its use." Within a few years, Gina had increased ankle distortion, although by this time she had received bracing from another rehabilitation center in New York City.

—The author worked with children with muscular dystrophy while a student therapist. We were informed that they would die in childhood. However, I worked with such individuals who lived into adulthood. Evidently they had not read the book that ordained their early deaths. But it was in their early years that these children developed joint and bone deformities, as well as muscle contractures, because of their inactivity. This led to irreversible deformities. Yet these were the types of deformities that could have been minimized by continuous physical activation, stretching, and range of motion (ROM) exercises.

Gina, and all of these children, fell victim to their classification as "severely and profoundly handicapped."

Each aspect of the disabilities of the multihandicapped, via *common* treatment modalities, responds to procedures offered by appropriate specific disability agencies. In our book we shall add our own approach and philosophy to those common procedures. Freed from the custodial context, it is a treatment method that has permitted hundreds of severely and profoundly handicapped to be served at last.

In the twenty-six-year history of the Institutes of Applied Human Dynamics, we have never dropped a client because of the severity of disability. It is from the methods and arts developed over those twenty-six years that we present our approach to the education, recreation, and habilitation of the severely and profoundly handicapped.

CHAPTER III

Disability

The etiology of disability (polio, malformation, hereditary agenesis, neoplasms, etc.) does not provide a useful starting point for those who make their contribution beyond the medical levels of intervention. A diagnosis may add to our knowledge of the totality of the condition but, to those of us who work in rehabilitation, education, and therapeutic recreation with the severely and profoundly handicapped, it is the *concept of disability* that provides us the reference points of *functional ability*. That is, it affords us the opportunity for establishing a level of function at a given point in time. It then allows us to measure or describe regression or improvement in changes from those points of function. Further, it permits us to offer specific methods for education and therapy that will modify or ameliorate the inability.

For example, what tactics are indicated for a child with hydrocephalus, once he has survived and has benefitted from medical care? Does a *diagnosis* of hydroencephalus necessarily tell us that he is retarded? Does it indicate that he has cerebral palsy or presents a behavior problem?

A description of the child's deficits, however, gives us some idea of what to look for and where to start. Is he blind, deaf, paretic, slow? Does he exhibit perceptual deficits, emotional problems, learning disabilities?

For the most part the severely and profoundly handicapped exhibit a lack of function or a dysfunction. Inabilities among the *developmentally disabled* may be:

1. due to a malgenesis or agenesis of a body part (in those children born without arms, eyes, eardrums, etc.);
2. due to a later loss of a body part or loss of function;
3. manifested by a lack of spontaneous reactivity and movement in relationship to events in the environment (failure to demonstrate developmental-stage-appropriate reflexes spontaneously);
4. manifested by a lack of spontaneous recovery after initial damage was sustained.

Some Functions That Are Manifested by Lack or Loss of Ability

Retardation

Retardation is an inability to be productive intellectually. Performance falls within a subnormal level of functioning. This condition begins in childhood and is still manifest at adulthood.

Subnormality is determined mainly by performance on a number of I.Q., adaptive appraisal, and social development tests. Subnormality (below 75 I.Q.) is evidenced when results fall below the area of scores achieved by the majority of test takers. As mentioned above, a person can be subnormal intellectually for a number of reasons: lack of brain capacity (hardest to demonstrate), social deprivation, or loss of access to information for a lengthy developmental period (due to blindness, deafness, other sensory impairments, perceptual gaps, etc.). People whose functioning is subnormal are often those with learning disabilities, emotional, or autistic qualities. Additionally, although other conditions such as mongoloidism and hydrocephalus correlate highly with low I.Q.'s, there are a significant number of people with above-normal I.Q.'s who have mongoloidism or hydrocephalus as a medical diagnosis.

Cerebral Palsy and Later Motor Impairment (Stroke)

Cerebral Palsy. This condition includes a broad range of functional impairments of motor and/or intellectual abilities. The most frequent types of motor impairments exhibited are:

1. Atonicity—lack of muscle tone.
2. Ataxia—tendency to fall.
3. Athetosis—a continuous thrashing movement.
4. Spasticity—tight, contracted muscles.
5. Tremor—continuous shaking.
6. Rigidity—tightness in both extensors and flexors.

Many persons with cerebral palsy or motor impairment at birth eventually merge into the normal population. Those who show some motor improveability, speech ability, or a degree of intellectual productivity are commonly served by agencies for the physically handicapped and/or the cerebral palsied. However, based on an expected speed of improveability, many cerebral palsied fail to develop speech or exhibit such "improveability" by age seven. They are then labelled "severely or profoundly handicapped," and are henceforth excluded from these services. Included in this category are those cerebral palsied who are also severely retarded, deaf, blind, or both; those who exhibit hyperactivity or behavior problems; and those with severe speech deficits.

Later Brain Damage. Those individuals who sustain sufficient damage in later life (due to stroke, tumor, trauma, infection), often exhibit many of the inabilities of the cerebral palsied. The more severely impaired—those who have sustained profound damage and show little or no recovery— often face the same categorizing and exclusion from services.

For example, recently we saw a thirty-six-year-old woman suffering from postencephalitis sequellae. For the past three years she had been in a custodial program in a hospital for the severe-chronic sick. She was now being evaluated, mainly by the TOWER* method, for a vocational diagnosis. Because of her ataxic syndrome and her problems with speech and coordination, it was assumed that she was functioning intellectually far below that indicated by her educational background. This woman had an associate degree in accounting, a bachelor's degree in education, and a master's degree in guidance.

Upon careful testing and through our experience with functional evaluations, we found this patient's college-level intellectual capacity intact and fully capable of functioning at this level. Her severe motor impairments did require rehabilitative intervention. At the time of this writing, this client continues to improve physically.

Autism

Autism is another functional category of disability. Its chief manifestations are an individual's apparent inability to respond, under ordinary conditions, to objects or persons in the environment, and difficulty with expressive language. Some autistic are hyperactive; some cannot make eye contact.

We rarely see young autistic children in our programs for the severely and profoundly handicapped. Because improveability is supposed to be manifest between the ages of seven and twelve, agencies for the emotionally disturbed and autistic do their finest work with children within this age bracket. After this period, however, the various programs exclude them as having adolescent problems of size, assertiveness, and aggression. Most agencies serving the autistic claim that they become disorganized in their later years and are better off in residential centers. They are reported as being unimproveable and more severely disturbed and thus are considered to be more unacceptable by society and professional workers,

It is the author's experience, however, that these older clients present a continuum of the same problems exhibited in childhood. Some improve with age while others are harder to deal with. This is especially so in larger individuals. In our experience many autistic learn to function in their later years. Some learn to speak in their late teens, and others start in their twenties.

*TOWER is a battery of tests used to evaluate work skills and is often used by vocational rehabilitation agencies. It was originally developed by ICD, the Institute for the Crippled and Disabled, Rehabilitation and Research Center, 340 East 24th Street, New York, New York 10010.

Too many of our service agencies and professionals want improveability to meet a time schedule. However, in our lifelong, day-to-day work with the autistic and others, we have seen that changes do occur. *Over a period of time, with the extension of activities, attention, and education, development and learning do take place.*

Emotional Disturbance

Emotional disturbances are dysfunctions of, or loss of affect—of feeling. Symptomatic of this problem, some children show moments of extreemly bizzare behavior, acting-up behavior, and often, withdrawal. Again, when children show a lack of improvement from seven to twelve years of age, they fall into the category of the severely handicapped and are recommended for institutional placement.

Other Inabilities

Other inabilities that can appear concurrent with major disabilities are incontinence, inability to feed oneself, inability to move, seizures, and impulsive behavior. Many of these are the consequences of the care given—disabilities secondary to inactivity and disuse. Withdrawal, hallucination, and fantasy will emerge in many children who are kept isolated, inactive, and away from a community of peers.

Induced Incontinence Some years ago, in one state institution in New York, patients were cared for by using a three-contiguous-buildings system. Children slept in Building One. They were then taken from their cribs and herded into Building Three where, without clothes, they were fed. Having no access to toilet facilities, they had to defecate on the floor. In late afternoon they were led into Building Two. Here they were showered down, dried, and had a gown thrown over them. They were then put to bed. Thus, semiambulatory children and adults from this building were thought to be incontinent.

After a short training period in a community program—in one instance less than one day—some of the adults appeared to have "learned to bowel-train and eat by themselves." It was apparent that they did not improve by new learning. Rather, they had probably had these skills earlier in life. Once institutionalized, however, they had adapted to their social system. What we would call regressed behavior was actually, given the social system of their institutional environment, adaptation and survival. If there is no access to a commode, or you are barred from access, where would you defecate?

Contractures. In another instance of secondary disability, patients over five feet in height presented contractures and distortions of the spine and legs. These were obvious manifestations of having to sleep for many years in cribs 4'10" long. Hunched over for so long, they developed spinal distortion, contractures, and bed sores.

Developmental Disabilities

The disabilities that we have been describing in this book are the atypical inabilities: those that demonstrate less improveability and modification in response to natural growth and development, and those that do not respond readily to current methods of treatment, rehabilitation, special education, or therapeutic recreation. The *developmental disabilities* are also inabilities that appear in infancy or childhood and attain at adulthood. They make the individual unable to respond wholly, at critical developmental periods, to some of the demands of the internal environment for growth. And at the same time, because of this dysfunction or inability, the external environment often fails to stimulate or elicit a developmental-appropriate response to its demands.

Innate Releasor Mechanisms (IRM's)

Normal development is a process that has its origins in the preconceptual stage. Inherited mechanisms are set into operation at conception. They become manifest via the growth and integration of these inherited mechanisms as they interact and intereffect each stage of their relationship to internal and external environments.

Once set into motion, a normally developing organism has its *inherited or innate releasor mechanisms (IRM's)* elicited by various inflections, deflections, and changes in the environment. Once released (imprinted), these mechanisms continue to function and grow, elaborate and integrate, in relation to the ongoing (ontological) environment.

For example, the mechanisms for breathing are inherited and are triggered an instant after birth. Mechanisms for hand movement, head turning, eye movement, etc., are all innate. Once released, they are strengthened by activity. Innate mechanisms become bound to events via contiguousness to reinforcement and functional relationship to the environment.

Developmentally disabled infants, in contrast to the normally developing infant, are characterized by the agenesis of some of these mechanisms, or the apparent inability of the environment to elicit the appropriate releasor mechanisms concurrent with the growth of the organism. Failure to elicit these IRM's at the critical time apparently affects the integration and elaboration of mechanisms.

This is particularly true as it affects motor, intelligence, perceptual, emotional, sensory, and the other higher functions. These higher functions are those that apparently come later to the individual, after his initial survival and after his early needs, such as breathing, feeding, and drinking, have been elicited.

The mechanisms involved in the higher functions are further elicited, molded, and changed by the family and community culture (the social environment) of the individual. This larger, more complex interplay with the inherited IRM's even further elaborates the integration of behavior with the environment.

IRM's and Development

For most individuals the elicitation of innate releasor mechanisms are in a context of caring individuals who respond to the needs and demands of the infant stage. The infant that is frequently held, grasped, warmed, rocked, changed, and fed lives in a social media that is continually changing. This creates an interactive stimulation of certain innate releasor mechanisms. These are elicited within the context of growth and they eventually integrate into the "developing child."

Where these mechanisms are impeded by malfunctioning parts (biochemical or biophysical), or by failure to develop in the first place (agenesis), important secondary mechanisms involved in the motor, intellectual, social, emotional, perceptual, and other such areas of development become impaired. This sequence then continues to affect the integration of these functions. If babies are not handled, rocked, and cuddled, important interactive mechanisms such as love and group-belonging fail to develop (Harlow). Even later, when these mechanisms can be elicited, the time of elicitation has forever affected the relation of these mechanisms to all new and future interactions with the environment.

This early lack of elicitation and interaction, and/or the dysfunction or nonfunctioning of organic components, form the basis for most developmental disabilities.

IRM's: Use and Disuse in the Evolution of Ability and Disability

Most IRM's are elicited as a consequence of inner need, social relations, or the mere interaction of the environment on the organism. The mechanisms are then strengthened and modified by their use and integration.

In developmentally disabled individuals, some of these mechanisms have not developed or are malfunctioning. Some cannot be elicited by ordinary changes in the environment because the cortical and humoral-chemical mechanisms for eliciting awareness and integration of external events are not functioning appropriately.

However, utilization of subcortical reflex mechanisms and exercise of malfunctioning systems can often get them going. Some can be elicited by special reflex techniques (discussed elsewhere in this book). If once elicited, the innate mechanisms can be started, integrated, and related to the growing organism.

All mechanisms (cortical, subcortical, spinal-reflexive) can lose their ability to integrate and elicit an action if permitted to go into disuse, whether initially elicited or not. Thus, *the mechanisms of integration are elicited by activity while disintegration takes place because of disuse. This is true for the normal as well as the disabled individual.*

At the Cellular Level. The form that cells take—their size and shape—are genetically determined and elaborated by the effect of their immediate environment. The permeability of the cell membrane is determined by the diet of the organism. The amounts of salt, sodium, or calcium, for instance, can determine the electrical quality (ionic state) of the cell wall. Based on these electrical qualities, it consequently accepts or rejects substances.

At the Level of Circulation. Development of the heart and circulatory system is related to the level of utilization of the system itself. The heart is a muscle and pumps more efficiently with exercise. The blood flows more efficiently as a result of exercise This affects its pressure in the capillaries and leads to an efficient carrying of oxygen and nutrients to the cells and elimination of waste from the cells. Sports medicine has amply demonstrated that there is a proliferation of capillaries in the periphery subsequent to activity and training. This results in efficient oxygenation of cells and organ systems and elaborates and makes more efficient the system carrying chemical messengers to the integrating systems.

As muscles contract, they press the blood back through venous capillaries and then through the semilunar valves of the veins. This allows for the return of waste from the cells and the return of the blood to the heart for oxygenation, along with the chemo-informational materials. Through activity and exercise blood is carried more efficiently to and from the kidneys, liver, brain, and other organs. Muscles lacking tone and periods of contraction cause a slow venous return, which can lead to venous and cardiac inefficiencies as well as behavior consequences of humoral-chemical imbalances.

Recent studies, using radioactive isotopes, of blood circulation to the brain have demonstrated that each body action has a number of correlative circulatory events occurring at various brain foci. This points out that body or organ activity is directly related to the specific utilization of brain centers, and that blood factors play a role in brain activity. Earlier research proved that disuse over extended periods of time of sensory stimulators sending messages to the brain resulted in diminution of cell growth, cell death, and degeneration of areas related to such stimulation, with commensurate degeneration of vascular mechanisms. (Lassen, Ingvar, and Skinhoj, 1978).

Current experimentation indicates that integrating mechanisms are not solely neurological. This is particularly so, since autonomic system organs do not have neurosensory (afferent) systems and are supplied only with effector (response) systems. Therefore, it is quite evident that humoral-chemical substances are part of the integrating systems; and sensory nerve endings, specializing in sensitivity to particular chemical substances and physical environmental changes, are integral to this integration system. For example, the brain, heart, and lungs do not have sensory mechanisms. They signal effect by throwing chemical messengers into the circulatory system. These are then reacted to by the whole organism.

Respiration. Exercise and activity lead to additional use of the muscles of respiration and the lungs, thus affecting their development, size, efficiency, and elasticity. A lung accustomed to exercise has a larger vital capacity (capacity to hold and exchange air and oxygen) than does an inactive lung. In addition, good oxygenation is directly correlated with the efficiency and strength of activity.

Using IRM's to Induce Normative Breathing in the Cerebral Palsied.
Persons with cerebral palsy often exhibit "tongue glottal breathing" (frog breathing), a form of breathing that fails to use much of the diaphragmatic and respiratory muscle structure involved in normal respiration. Apparently an example of a developmental arrest of respiratory function, the IRM's for diaphragmatic and respiratory muscle breathing were not, for some reason, elicited at birth. As the child grows older, the additional lack of stimulation and development of the higher systems will usually result in her becoming fixed in glottal breathing.

In normal individuals there exists a process of *reverse breathing,* a survival mechanism should the individual suddenly experience a serious decrease in his air supply. During normal respiration, the slightly higher pressure of gases inside the lungs forces oxygen into the blood stream, to be distributed to the tissues, while it allows carbon dioxide into the lungs to be exhaled as waste. Reverse breathing involves a build-up of the oxygen inside the lungs as well as an increasing accumulation of the carbon dioxide that was not exhaled. Pressure continues to increase in the lungs and the carbon dioxide levels in the blood also increase. Finally, this situation trips off the following sequence:

1. Ever greater pressure from the accumulated gases is exerted on the lungs to *force* exhalation:

2. The higher carbon dioxide levels in the blood stimulate certain chemoreceptors which, in turn, trigger potentials for the diaphragmatic and respiratory muscle reflex function that had been interrupted.

Reverse breathing in an emergency situation thus restores equilibrium and reestablishes normal respiration in the average individual.

For the cerebral palsied with tongue glottal breathing, we have successfully employed the same principles active in the above survival situation. Utilizing the same innate mechanisms, we then stimulate the higher system reflexly, thus inducing a normal breathing pattern for these clients, often for the first time in their lives. The child is able to breathe more efficiently as the process becomes well developed and maintained. Since the constant tongue movement is now also under control, the child's drooling stops and speech becomes clearer. Take, for example, the following situation:

Lottie, an eight-year-old child, was a quadriparetic. spastic, cerebral palsied girl with glottal breathing. At the first of a dozen sessions in the swimming pool, her head was lowered face down into the water for about two to three seconds. By lifting her entire head and shoulders in a horizontal plane, care was taken that her nose and mouth were submerged and lifted out exactly at the same moment. This prevented a "swallowing reflex" from taking over. Rather than swallow water, Lottie reflexively held her breath, an innate reflex mechanism from an early developmental stage.

As we increased the time under water by two seconds after each five trials, Lottie began to develop a more normal breathing pattern, including breath holding. At 30 to 45 seconds of submersion, she began to hold and release her breath rhythmically. By thus stimulating the innate mechanisms for survival, reverse breathing, she began to develop and strengthen the mechanisms and muscles involved in diaphragmatic and respiratory muscle breathing. Eventually Lottie was able to maintain the normal breathing pattern permanently, her drooling stopped, and her speech improved.

We have had similar successful experiences with several other cerebral palsied clients. All had originally been using tongue glottal breathing. Each one eventually learned to breathe and swallow normally and speak more fluently.

Bone. Bone develops according to function. Its ability to take strain, bear weight, have elasticity and a certain structure is related to its use. A properly used bone is structurally and functionally different from a bone in disuse. Much of the bone distortion we see in the developmentally handicapped is related to disuse—positions taken for long periods of time without change.

Bone in a state of disuse loses its living quality (bone death). Bone cells and the organic calcium structures break down. Thus we see such a condition as osteoporosis with its resultant bone weakness, brittleness, and fractures.

Joints. The development of the joint is related to its utilization during the developmental stages. The ability of a joint capsule to support a body position is often related to its use and disuse. Furthermore, a disused joint is often infiltrated with fibers and becomes ankylosed (bony), which prevents further movement.

Nerve. The development of the size of a nerve and its connections is also related, in part, to its use and disuse. An exercised nerve is wider—it has more neuroplasm and carries messages more quickly than a disused nerve. The quantity of transmitter substance is related to the frequency of firing at a nerve ending; in turn, the speed of a message crossing from one nerve to another is related to the quantity and quality of neuroplasm. The connections in the nerves of axons to dendrites is achieved and disconnected in relation to use and disuse. Therefore, a utilized system is more swift and more efficient then an underutilized one.

Muscle. The volume of myoplasm and the size of muscle fibers are also related to whether or not a muscle fiber is used. The size and elasticity of the muscle and its chemistry bear directly on the ability of a muscle to contract or to sustain tension and activity. This affects the organism's ability to do anything from changing position and posture to performing work. It also affects the proper return of blood to the heart for oxygenation as well as to the other systems for nutrients and elimination of waste.

Constancy and Constant Environmental Conditions

It appears that constancy and lack of stimulation in any setting results in the development of increased hyperactivity, random behavior, and movement in some individuals, and complete lack of activity and movement in others. While working with some thirty Willowbrook clients in a day treatment program, most of whom had a history of such behavior and symptoms, we observed a tremendous and immediate moderation of hyperactivity and acting up. This was subsequent to their being programmed for a long treatment day: three hours of travel per day, six hours of program, and two hours of preparation before going to the program. The mere involvement in a long program day significantly modified their overall behavior. Eventually, these clients required less intense management and functioned with greater capability in their more restrictive, residential setting at Willowbrook.

In Conclusion

Disability can be the consequence of a malgenesis or agenesis of innate mechanisms, later trauma, or infection.

However, much of what we now consider to be characteristics of severe and profound disability are in reality secondary to inactivity—to disuse that is usually the result of a lack of attention to and correction of the initial (true) disability. Similar disuse can cause or increase disability in higher functioning persons and render them severely distorted physically or severely disturbed emotionally and socially. Thus, they also become the severely and profoundly handicapped.

Our succeeding discussion shall be devoted to our methods for ameliorating primary disability and for preventing secondary disability due to inactivity and resultant disuse. Our program of eliciting maximal activity and function by spontaneous means, strengthening that activity through voluntary exercise or rehearsal, and intervention, using reflexive or induced action, can prevent further disability.

CHAPTER IV

Principles For Habilitation, Education, and Recreation For the Severely and Profoundly Handicapped. The Time and Place For Program

Until recently, the concept of the severely and profoundly handicapped has been defined by the absence of habilitation and educational services available to them. Because these handicapped are labeled severe and profound, they are not included in physical therapy programs, are not accepted into special education programs in schools, and are excluded from services of the day and residential treatment services. Instead they have been either kept at home or stored in custodial warehouses by the hundreds, places devoid of little more than feeding, toileting, and basic nursing services.

Who, then, are to serve them?

—*The psychologists* who defined them as severely and profoundly retarded?

—*The physical therapists* who accepted their inactivity and waited for spontaneous development to take place?

—*The teachers* who only yesterday excluded them from their classrooms as unteachable?

—*The professors* who teach the teachers and who once claimed these handicapped to be beyond treatment?

And where and when should the severely and profoundly handicapped be served?

—In the public schools?

—In special education classes?

—In recreation programs?

—During the day?

—In the evenings?

—On weekends?

—When?

After twenty-five years of work with the severe and profoundly handicapped, we have come to a number of conclusions:

The severe and profoundly handicapped are a *multihandicapped* lot. They have *combinations* of neurological, emotional, sensory, intellectual, and perceptual disabilities.

Persons who work with the multihandicapped must have a broad, general knowledge of psychophysiology, neurophysiology, psychology, social development, education, learning and behavior theories; they must possess recreation, activity, teaching, and many other skills.

Each unit of service to the multihandicapped must possess individuals who are not only generalists, versed in all of the above arts and skills, but who are, additionally, trained specialists (teachers, physical therapists, nurses, etc.). Equipped with such a background, the workers can integrate all these skills and apply them through their specialized efforts to the unique and individual problems of each client. At the same time, they can instruct other workers in these techniques.

Over the past twenty years we have never met a person with only a university education in any field who was sufficiently prepared to render service to the severely or profoundly handicapped. On the other hand, we have given college-level seminars and on-the-job training to those people with excellent technical knowledge and skills but who lacked a formal university education. This gave them the ability to apply the arts and techniques they now possessed to new clients, in new situations. Thus, in our work with the multihandicapped, theory and practice are inherent to each other.

Staff and Workers

Although, as we stated earlier, almost every worker must be a generalist, there are special roles, skills, and areas of achievement that are important in our work. For example:

1. *The Parent* acts as the source of information, the central figure in home care; the most powerful political advocate and, in many cases, organizer of services and new resources for care. Often a volunteer or paid worker, she meets with and reports to the staff, and receives their reports in turn. When it is convenient she can assume any of the treatment roles. Here, possessing those special qualities as a parent, she can be especially effective.

2. *The Social Worker* assembles past medical, social, psychological, and other clinical information. He or she meets with and reports to the staff, acts as integrator of services to the family and as the liaison between agencies.

3. *The Physician/Pediatrician* requests clinical material and more detailed explorations of clinical services rendered. He or she refers clients for medical follow-ups and makes medical recommendations to the client's physical treatment agency. The physician also reviews treatment plans, medication records, and meets with and reports to the staff.

4. *The Psychiatrist* evaluates clinical records and the client in relation to dysfunctions of affect and perception. He or she also refers clients back to their own treatment physicians or agencies.

5. *The Psychologist* gives psychometric and psychodynamic tests, interviews parents and works with children and teachers on learning tasks and modification of behavior. He reviews the clinical records and integrates them into all programs as they apply to the client. He, too, meets with and reports to the staff.

6. *The Communicologist* reviews the client's history regarding perceptive abilities and deficits and determines the avenues of communication and speech available to each client. He or she meets with staff members to instruct them on specific techniques of communication with each child.

7. *Directing Teachers, Supervising Teachers, and Other Administrative Staff* audit the quality and quantity of service to be given to each class and to each child. They review the individual lesson plans and instruct each teacher and worker in the techniques, methods, and programs to be used. They also interpret the test indicating psychological, language, perceptual and/or physical deficits; coordinate this information with the program; and guide the development and implementation of activities to ameliorate the deficits.

8. *Special Education Teachers* plan out the curriculum in conjunction with the supportive staff. They devise an individualized prescriptive educational, social, and physical education program addressed to the special needs of each child. They also integrate the supportive systems into a graded educational program for each of their student workers, aides, and volunteers.

9. *Adaptive Physical Education Teachers* develop programs for gross activities and games to strengthen gross motor skills, coordination, and balance. They also develop programs to enhance fine motor skills, rhythm, and coordination, and they assist teachers to integrate these programs into the academic setting.

10. *Child Development Workers* concentrate mainly on initiating physical activity, early socialization, games, activities of daily living, and eating skills. They are skilled in using individualized behavior modification techniques.

11. *The Therapeutic Recreationist* utilizes prescriptive activity forms and game skills on an after-school and after-hours basis. This service attempts to develop physical coordination, strength, and ability to endure stress, social change, and interaction; eventually to endure a working day. The therapeutic recreationist also attempts to develop in the client the ability to enjoy leisure time activities, and the experience of relaxation, joy, and a sense of well-being.

12. *The Occupational Educator* elicits purposeful activities from the beginning. These are gradually related to such purposeful productive work as kitchen skills, clerical work and janitorial activities. Actual sub-contract work is eventually undertaken. Our Work Activity Center serves clients aged seventeen and over.

The Time for the Programs

Day training and treatment assignments usually run weekdays, 8:30 A.M. to 2:30 P.M.; prevocational and additional physical activation and tutorial work, 2:30 A.M. to 5:00 P.M. Then, there is a therapeutic recreation and games program from 5:00 to 7:00 P.M. Additional programs are also offered on Saturdays and Sundays. On Fridays, the programs are extended to 10:00 P.M.; on Saturdays the program runs until 10:30 P.M.

A client or his family can take all or part of the services offered, depending on the prescriptive needs of the child and his family to utilize what is offered.

In our experience, the optimum time for teaching a skill may be any time during an activity day—during busing, eating, swimming, games, toileting, occupational educaton. The longer day and varied functional activities afford diagnostic information and increase the opportunity for ongoing prescription of activity to modify problems as they actually present themselves. In the same way, a counseling session may be most effective when the counselor and child are hanging off the side of a pool or sitting together at the dinner table. The best time for a service to be given, therefore, is when a client is highly motivated and most receptive. The exceptional nature of the dysfunctions require our openness to unusual time arrangements and opportunities for learning.

The Principles of the Program

When one of our teachers complains of a child defecating in his clothes, or of another child acting up, we remind that teacher of the primary principle of our program: Clients are never excluded from the program because of the severity of their problem or disability. (But teachers will leave, often before they have given themselves a chance to learn what to do).

The second principle of our program is: activity, movement, and stimulation are vital to the amelioration and modification of all disability. Every client must be stimulated, induced to move when he cannot move independently, and involved in prescriptive purposeful activity when he cannot involve himself autonomously. Unwanted behavior, hyperactivity, and random movement must be inhibited or aversively conditioned if it prevents a client from learning or participating in purposive activity.

CHAPTER V

The Development of Activity
Of the Nervous System

The nature, shape, and form of organismic development is determined from preconception by an inherited genetic plan. The course and character of development, however, is affected by an interplay of internal and external environmental forces acting on the developing protoplasm. Thus, the structure of a cell is only an expression of the responses of the developing cell to its environment.

In the environment of the maternal media (the womb), the growing fetus is engulfed by a rather constant level of moisture, warmth, and darkness. This environment provides a steady supply of available chemical nutrients from the mother's system and serves as an egress for waste. Thus oxygen exchange, elimination, and all activities necessary for life are provided for. Changes in the chemical or physical balance (homeostasis) interacting on growing mechanisms affect further growth and development.

Throughout the entire life of an organism, a change in the chemical environment affects the ionic nature of the semipermeable membranes of the cells. What is accepted or rejected at the cell membrane level is related to its ionic relationship to its environment. Another aspect of change that affects growing relationships can be described by the piezoelectric phenomena effect. This occurs when any organic substances of two different ionic charges pass each other or are subjected to stress, compression, elasticity, thermal changes, or changes in water content. Examples would be: bone being used as levers or supports for standing or twisting; muscles when they are stretched and rewound, thus winding and unwinding the muscle fiber helix; and increases or decreases in the internal or surrounding temperatures of the organism. This same phenomena effect holds true for inorganic substances that have ionic qualities. The piezoelectric phenomena effect is the result of one or more of the above events and causes a change in the ionic or electrical relationship between cells, their immediate environment, and the larger environment.

These electrochemical phenomena affect the normal daily maintenance of cellular life and are the essence of that condition we call "life." This electrical activity occurs when bone is used through activities such as stress, stretching, torsion, bone strain. An electric pump operates to pull nutrients and oxygen into the osteocytes (bone cells) and to push out waste matter and carbon dioxide. Failure of these bone pumps to operate results in bone death. A lack of bone use affects the quality and longevity of the bone. And should this pump system fail, an even more far-reaching effect of bone death is the failure to produce bone marrow.

The bone marrow is the site for the development of blood cells. As bone death progresses, the production of red blood cells diminishes. Thus respiration, oxygenation, and energization of the whole organism are affected. Concurrent with a diminished red blood cell production, protective white cell production becomes insufficient and lowers the resistance of the organism to infection.

Studies of inactivity regarding the physiological effect of the piezoelectrical phenomena have substantiated the above theories. For example, the results of inactivity have been noted in persons who contracted polio and were subjected to prolonged periods of rest. These studies have demonstrated that such individuals have shown a substantial loss of bone mass after extended bed rest. This same condition was noted in astronauts after orbital flights. In 1965, the astronauts in Gemini IV lost between one and twelve percent of bone mass in their hands and feet by the end of their four-day mission. The astronauts of Gemini V experienced a loss of twenty percent of bone mass during an eight-day mission. This loss was due to the lack of activity and the effect of the absence of gravity. However, the astronauts of Gemini VI and Gemini VII were given exercises to reduce the loss of bone mass. It was concluded that the elecrical pump phenomena, driven by the stress, strain, and torsion of exercise, was able to effect the maintenance of bone mass.

Along the same lines of investigation, growth data revealed a dependence of growth rate on muscular exercise. Studies have demonstrated that a larger quantity of energy is expended in the lying and quadriped position than in the standing position. Muscle activity also utilizes body energy at a greater level of efficiency than does a muscle in the inactive state. In addition, muscle activity is integral to enzyme and organ function at each developmental stage.

The above is true of respiratory, cardiovascular, excretory, and digestive systems. All are affected structurally by the demands of activity or the results of inactivity. The size and volume of work performed by each organ during long periods of activity and inactivity is directly related to its development.

Thus the chemistry, growth, and maintenance of living cells and tissues affects the development of structure in individuals and determines how the hereditary plan will be elaborated. Structure, development, and longevity, although genetically programmed, depend on cycles of activity and inactivity for their elaboration.

The Sensory System

There have been a number of studies that have demonstrated the relationship of activity to levels of brain activity. In some of these studies, parts of the brain were completely isolated (in situ) from surrounding brain tissue. Encephalographic records showed that there was an absence of activity in those areas that had been isolated and had received no input. When these same areas were stimulated electrically, wave activity was recorded emanating from the cells. Thus cortical activity is not spontaneous but must be elicited by afferent input (input from the environment).

Another group of experiments left a few of the afferent fibers intact in those sections that had been isolated. Results of testing showed that the amount the cortical activity was directly related to the number of afferent fibers left intact.

Possible differences in behavior may be traced to the development of the nervous system, from its earliest moment of conception through its whole prenatal stage. When the embryo reaches the blastophore stage, ectodermal cells, lying in the mid-dorsal line, move forward and thicken to form a neural plate. The neural plate then depresses medially to form a neural groove. This neural groove closes over dorsally, resulting in a neural tube that extends the full length of the embryo and becomes evaginated anteriorly into the brain. The neural tube then sinks below the embryonic surface and forms the root structure of the adult nervous system. The nervous system develops from this root structure.

Cells begin to migrate outwards from the root structure to form ganglia and nerves. These then take over control of the organs. At this point, it is essential that we stop and understand the implications of this migration.

The nerve elements found in the neonate muscles, for example, do not develop in the muscles themselves. Rather, they develop in the neural tube and migrate out later to become secondarily associated with the nervous system (Hauber, 1949). By the time this occurs, the organs of the body are fairly well developed and some of them are quite active (e.g., the embryonic heart and kidneys).

Myogenic responses, i.e., earliest behavior, precede reflexes in the mammal (Windle, 1940). Reflexes do not manifest themselves until efferent neurons develop. These simple nerve endings appear in peripheral tissues and connect them to the central nervous system by the formation of functional synaptic mechanisms.

Further, Windle stated that discrete movements are not the primary units of behavior. Rather, local reflexes are differentiated from a more fundamental background of massive movement. He demonstrated that muscle contractions could be induced by a discharge of motor neurons even before reflex arcs were completely formed. Reflex responses to stimulation are manifested when conduction first takes place; stimuli are processed from afferent to efferent neurons through the synaptic centers. This event marks the genesis of the development of integrated behavior (Ibid.).

If we postulate the interference of abnormal influences during this period, we can begin to understand the occurrence of developmental anomalies and nerve function imperfections. Conditions such as bacterial invasions, toxoplasmosis, and infections affect the physiochemical environment and produce changes in the ionic environment of the organism. Because the physiochemical guides have been altered during the outward migration of neurons, information is thereafter transmitted that produces maldevelopment of nerve function, or even blocks its development (agenesis).

Let us examine this process in greater detail. As Windle's (1940) experiments have shown, relatively simple innate reflex responses are the basic elements in the genesis of mammalian behavior. The more integrated and complex reactions of the older fetus are formed by a progressive neuronal integration of less complicated activities of the embryo.

The earliest secondary neurons of the spinal cord build pathways that are essentially ascending. Those of the automatic nervous system even at maturity, in contrast, are essentially descending. It is an effector system without ascending neural communication. (However, there is humoral communication via the circulatory system.) Until spinal cord responses are established, the descending tracts of the developing brain send few fibers into the spinal cord. All nervous elements essential for reflex action are present in the embryonic cord. Intrinsic synaptic connections are being stimulated directly, prior to the appearance of reflex-like responses (Ibid.), and prior to the higher level and cortical integration.

The appearance of the reflexes marks the next step in behavioral development, after the appearance of afferent and efferent neurons and synaptic mechanisms. The reflexes, advanced levels of behavior, develop through a process of individualization from a fully integrated, mass reaction of "total pattern." Discrete and specialized reflexes rather than single fine movements are the original units of behavior. The mechanisms of their development are genetically determined and are elaborated, as functions of time, as each reflex is released (the initial elicitation of the IRM's) (Ibid.).

Early studies believed that all neurons any organism will ever possess were present at a very early stage of fetal development. And Strauss (1948) stated that an injury or infection at any point in prenatal development affects the organism so that future growth periods are never the same. However, if the physiology and conditioning of reflexes is understood, some factors influencing reflex development can be effected in later life by training. New studies have shown that new synapses are formed throughout life, depending upon the variety and intensity of stimuli received by the individual. For example, if light is prevented from stimulating the eyes of a young dog for an extended period of time, adjustor neurons in the optic lobe do not grow or transmit information in the usual manner.

Weiss and Hiscoe (1948) reported experiments that confirmed earlier reports of growth in neural tissue after birth. They demonstrated that neuroplasm is constantly being formed from the nuclear territory of the neuron, and is then pushed down the axon sheaths. The neuron, if not overloaded, reacts immediately with increased synthesis. The cell can shrink or swell as much as forty percent in this process (Jeffress, 1951).

The Weiss and Hiscoe findings demonstrated that brain cell size and brain volume are affected by the use-disuse phenomena. Their studies of mechanisms of volume, connections, and disconnections have given us a physiological and structural demonstration of how a connection takes place: each stimuli results in a trace increment of neuroplasmic volume and a change in transmitter substance. This influences the connections or disconnections. It is not until late in fetal life that the cerebral cortex exerts any influence over the lower motor parts of the nervous system. And the pyramidal (fine motor) tracts are the last to be formed.

The Development of Behavior

The behavior mechanisms of various organisms are different primarily because of the differences in their interactive systems. In the simplest unicellular organism it is an impact of external energy which affects the state of the plasma membrane. The action of the environment on this organism alters the state of the membrane and affects its selectivity to various materials around it. This, in turn, affects its internal balance.

In the course of evolution (phylogenesis), the sense organisms have developed by being in intimate contact with movement to or from external objects (Granit, 1955). In the unicellular organisms the effect of external objects impinges directly on the cell. In multicellular organisms, the action of an external object is projected to the component cells of the organism via varios types of conduction systems. These elicit reactions in other cells of the organism. In the porifera, for example, actions in the external environment are transmitted from cell to cell. In higher organisms such as the worm and crustaceans, external environmental actions are conducted more rapidly, via specialized elongated neurons, rather than from cell to cell.

Climbing yet higher on the phylogenetic ladder, we find the development of behavior mechanisms consisting of ever more complex conduction systems eventually forming into what might be called a primitive brain. All the essential features of earlier conduction and reaction systems are retained, but the development of the brain is now closely related to the relationship that the organism has with its environment. For example, the basal ganglia develops in relation to that of the limbs and swift muscle movement. The cerebellum develops in relation to the mode of locomotor activity of an organism, and its size appears to be related to the swiftness of movement. The slow-moving carp and sluggish sheep each have smaller cerebellums than the mobile salmon and the horse. The cerebellum reaches its peak development in primates.

Beginning with primitive organisms, therefore, the brain develops into three basic regions:

1. The forebrain—from which develop the olfactory lobes, cerebral hemispheres, and pineal body.

2. The midbrain—from which develop a pair of optic lobes.

3. The hindbrain—which differentiates into a cerebellum and a medulla.

The ganglia are retained as aspects of the spinal cord and the peripheral system (Hauber, 1949).

In fish, amphibia, reptiles, and birds the differentiated regions are present, but the cortical mantle of the cerebellum is absent or rudimentary. The corpus striatum, one of the oldest parts of the cerebellum, is the highest motor center. The actions of the lower organisms are characterized by massive coordinated actions, but the environments that these organisms can act on and react to are still limited when compared to mammals. Fish are bound to the sea, amphibia must have access to certain climates and to water to bear young, and primates are native to jungles.

As life achieves higher forms, the pyramidal system comes into being coincidentally or concurrently with the organism's ability to move in and manipulate the environment. Concurrent with this growing ability is the development of the cerebral cortex. In the mammalian brain, and most conspicuously in the human, the anterior regions grow into an enormous cerebrum. Again, the functions of the lower systems are not lost, nor are all those of the extrapyrmidal systems, since they carry out the automatic reflex movements concerned with maintaining posture and the ability to mobilize the organism for action. Man still responds by reflex to the mechanisms of hunger, fear, anger, and fright. But only man can live for extended periods of time in all climates and environments including outer space.

Man senses and feels through cells in the cerebral cortex and perceives only those stimuli that present themselves to these cells. Impulses may reach motor cells in the cerebral cortex after passing through subcortical structures; or, they may arrive via new pathways, bypassing older systems, or by way of sensory organs.

In the absence of afferent impulses there is little spontaneous motor cortex discharge. As we have said, reflexes do not manifest themselves until the afferent and efferent neurons (simple nerve endings in the peripheral tissue) and connector neurons in the central nervous system have been developed. Thus, there appears to be a direct connection between incoming levels of stimulation and the later "spontaneous" activity. Action needs input from the afferent sensory system as a prior condition for altering the ideational areas of the effector systems.

Activity in the central nervous system seems to be related to the development of the cells' size, synaptic connections, and conductor tracts. Conversely, disuse raises the threshhold of readiness of the cerebral cells to react (Cajal, 1952). This results in diminished cell size development, less transmitter substance, fewer synaptic connections, and less development in the conductor tracts.

Defects in Development

Developmental defects can arise in the process of fetal growth. These defects may be found at many levels of severity. For example, closure of the neural tube is followed by proliferation of cells in the germinal layer, which subsequently migrate to more lateral portions of the nervous system. Should closure fail to occur in portions of the neural tube, as frequently happens, further development of the involved nervous tissue will be deficient.

In the process of migration, certain groups of cells may be left behind. These will develop normally, but in an abnormal position. In addition, those areas derived from a single part of the neural tube may fail to mature, remaining in a primitive state. Or they may fail to develop at all (agenesis). The appearance of any of these defects depends on the developmental state of the embryo in which the deviation occurs, the size of neural tube or the amount of its derivatives affected, and the intensity of the entire process (Grinker, 1951).

Homeostasis and Activity

The organism also retains mechanisms of action and reaction which antedate the development of electrical conduction systems (the nervous system). The action and reaction of these elecrical conduction systems include all the earlier modes as part of the more advanced processes.

All activities of life are initiated, mediated, and maintained by the dynamic interrelationship of chemical and physical processes. Pulse rate and pressure, bone hardening, irritability, conductivity, eating, thinking, and reproduction—all the processes of life—are means by which the organism responds to and adapts to its environment; and all are products of this dynamic interrelationship.

The living body is an energy system acting to maintain a state of equilibrium. A change in the internal or external environment becomes a stimulus which causes change in this equilibrium. This change in balance influences the state of the organism and initiates body activity so that the change may be accounted for. The action that achieves a new state of equilibrium is performed under the command of the central nervous system.

The neuromotor system adjusts the body in relation to its external environment. The autonomic system adjusts the organism to its internal environment. Its parasympathetic component system maintains and conserves, and its sympathetic system meets emergency situations.

Uniformity and stability in normal body states is maintained by the blood of the organism (Dorland, 1947). But the structural and functional integration of the organismic system is determined by the ongoing interaction of internal and external factors. This integration antedates the nervous system both phylogenetically and ontogenetically (Freeman, 1948). It exists as a concurrent and integral system of humoral integrating mechanisms in the intact organism.

In denervated structures we see a return to this primitive level of maintenance in order to preserve life (Cannon, 1949). The efficiency and longevity of higher organisms, however, are dependent on the coordination of the central nervous system. In all intact individuals, neuro- or humoral systems interact to govern all body functions. Humoral chemical systems appear early in fetal development and form into a neurohumoral system, predating the more advanced stage of a true nervous system. Functions of a nervous system are finally carried out by integrated humoral-neural tissue, under the command of the nervous system.

Homeostasis is the theoretical chemical or physical point at which balance is reached. Normal activity is based upon minute variations in these systems and stems from the attempt to reach balance. If this balance were reached and maintained, all body activities would cease. However, since the organism is a dynamic system, fluctuations in balance occur continuously and the body acts and reacts in response. These fluctuations can be brought about by activity, inactivity, and the passing of time itself.

A stimulus is some change in the environment, but the intensity and response to a stimulus is based upon the amount and type of imbalance it creates. Intensity will be limited if there is a quick, automatic compensation. But if balance cannot be achieved locally, more and more of the body's action and reaction mechanisms are activiated to return it to balance (Spread of Effect). An example would be the difference in the body's response to a local infection, such as a boil, and its response to a generalized empyema. Another example would be unsatisfied food needs initiating aggressive behavior. And stimuli from unsatisfied sexual needs can reach the limbic system. By spread of effect, this results in sublimation of behavior, as cortical and subcortical centers are eventually activated that were not originally recruited.

Additionally, if an external stimulus is applied to a point in the body it will cause an increase of the metabolic rate at that point. The effect of this soon radiates throughout the body and then decreases as, sooner or later, excitation produces more or less permanent changes in protoplasmic structure and action (Freeman, 1948). The application of heat, for example, causes a local erythema. Soon, vasoconstriction then dilation proceed throughout the entire periphery via a nervous mechanism. The entire body will experience changes (Landis-Gibbons effect). If the heat stimulus is continued a burn will occur at the site of stimulation. Similarly, the ionic qualities of direct current, when applied to a body part, will affect the entire body. However, recognizable protein coagulation (acid reaction) will be observed at the positive pole.

If the reaction is not elicited and the stimulus is held constant, we have habituation. That is, such stimuli, given a constant condition, will not be responded to at a given threshhold. Therefore, phylogenetically, as soon as qualitative differences in protoplasmic structure or function appear at different levels, specialized integrating mechanisms (vascular and nervous systems) will begin to take over the task of coordinating the organism as a unified whole (autogenetically). Structural changes in nerve tissue also occur, such as increased capillary circulation to certain nerve fibers in response to their new activity levels.

Fatigue

Fatigue is a phenomenon of imbalance of the body and occurs when intake and output of biological energy is not equalized. The cells and organs of the body, having undergone excessive activity, are unable to maintain their full capacity to respond to a stimulus. It is associated with weariness and overexertion (Schneider, 1939) and is a phenomenon of all body tissues.

Muscle tissue and neural tissue differ in their fatigability. Since nerve tissue recovers more rapidly, the motor fatigue accumulation in the total organism comes from the muscle tissue. There is considerable evidence that renewed command of motor apparatus can take place under a change of afferent stimulation. This can be explained by the fact that new afferent pathways that command the previously unused and unfatigued muscle fibers are really motor nerve responses to the new source of stimulation. New vascular connections bring blood and renewed oxygen supply to active muscle fibers, and effect neurochemical increases in efficiency and change.

Fatigue serves an important function in that an organism avoids repetition of identical responses; it will cease to respond to continued repetitive stimulation of the same order. Only stimuli of a higher intensity (threshold) can then become liminal during a partially refractory period. This constant condition is called *habituation*.

The Genesis of Activity

Interaction in an organic field, by its very nature, is characterized by action and counteraction. Activity at various strata of life (chemical, phpysiological, sociopsychological, etc.) causes the organism to develop along more organized and epigenetic lines. When the action of the internal mechanism increases the organismic field of action and reaction to the external environment (within the limits of organismic safety), there is also an increase of field counteraction and reaction. When the actions of external mechanisms increase their field action and reaction and cause an increase in the activity of the internal mechanisms of an organism, there appears to be an acceleration of epigenetic development. This is the organism's ability to organize and derive what it needs in the environment, or to adapt to change in a forward moving or advancing direction. The epigenesis of development can be demonstrated on both phylogenetic and ontogenetic continuums.

In the most primitive phyla, a change in the chemical or physical state of the internal media results in rapid movement. For example, when a paramecium is put into a food-deprived environment it begins to move rapidly. Its movement, although random, results in its covering large distances. When food is introduced into the media, the paramecium's swift, rapid, and random actions result in frequent collisions with objects until, finally, it collides with a food object. It then slows down or stops in order to propel the food with its cilia toward its oral groove.

The action of the paramecium in the food-deprived environment can be assumed to be a result of an internal action and reaction causing an action on the environment. There was nothing in the environment to exert a force on the paramecium.

An introduction of an acid or base, however, into an area of the water media of the paramecium results in its swimming rapidly away from that area. Thus the chemical activity of the external environment will cause a unicellular organism to move away from this aversive force. This action is epigenetic—a connection occurs and the organism can adapt to a situation. In the future, the paramecium can avoid an irritant by merely moving away.

Another example would be when an obstacle exerts force on an amoeba. This propels the amoeba in the direction of the sol. This substance forms when the amoeba's pseudopod strikes an obstacle. The cytoplasm in that region then begins to turn to gel and sol begins to form in the opposite direction. Finally, the amoeba backs away in the direction of the sol. Thus, by this action, the amoeba moves clear of the obstacle.

The internal action of both of these unicellular organisms is quite primitive; the moving toward is caused by a chemical or physical state which moves it at random through its environment. When, either by contact or collision, something impinges on the organism, it moves away in a random fashion until the obstacle is avoided.

We can observe epigenetic development as we move up the phylogenetic scale. Organisms will have increasingly more organized and numerous internal mechanisms for finding substances in the environment to satisfy internal needs and for recognizing and avoiding irritants and obstacles. The initial inherited systems we see operating here are called the Innate Releasor Mechanisms—the IRM's.

Epigenetically we find, finally, the development of light-sensitive and sound-sensitive organisms. These properties allow for the quicker development and more rapid action on the internal states. The action and reaction of the internal mechanisms will be swifter to propel the organism toward or away from substances and objects in its environment. Also, there will be a more rapid action and reaction to the environment— substances and events are "picked up" by the organism with less random action. This reflects epigenetic development. An organism can move rapidly and definitely to adapt to situations. It appears that, at this level, experience is stored in a "chemical memory." Actions, having formed neurological components, are now physiochemical in nature. As we rise higher on the phylogenetic ladder, we begin to observe a form of memory and objectification. When an object or situation is experienced, the organism can make decisions as to whether or not it will move toward or away from it. Internal states have been established by trace experiences and now exert a force on the direction of an action or reaction.

We note, also, that experience seems to have an ontogenetic component. That is, very little action or reaction is exerted in a predetermined manner until the organism experiences the behavior, or until it is more organized, less random and thus, more epigenetic. Going down the phylogenetic scale, there is relatively more primitive and less adaptive action and reaction. We encounter an organism with less storage of ontogenetic traces experience (memory). But as phylogenetic and ontogenetic stages advance, the swift, random actions of the younger organisms result in an accumulation of trace experiences. There is a progressive lessening of random action and reactions and an increased coordination, purposiveness, and adaptability of the organism's actions and reactions to internal needs and external objects and relations.

In higher organisms, action and reaction seem to be still more purposive. That is, actions decrease the frequency of collision with objects in the environment. This results in a learned reaction. The organism now either moves toward and engulfs or rejects and moves away from these once-experienced objects.

The epigenesis of experience (memory) and the consequent reduction of random, nonpurposive actions and reactions is related to *the frequency of this encounter rehearsal*. Each encounter sets up a trace record of the event. Additional encounters result in additional traces, recordings, modifications, corrections, and changes. It is now thought that memory causes short- and long-term changes—short-term memory (stm) and long-term memory (ltm). Therefore, phylogenetic and ontogenetic factors play a role in the development of purposive behavior.

The very nature of a living organism causes it to act and move about to satisfy its needs. It is able to receive and react to obstacles, record experiences, and, thus, be able to react and adapt accordingly. The more sedentary the organism the less will inherited behavior continue to be modified by experiences. This makes the organism less capable of adaptation to changing situations, new obstacles, and new objects. Activity, therefore, is essential to the development of experience. It determines the level and manner in which an organism will act, react, and interact with its environment. It is the essence of behavior itself.

Postnatal Development of Cerebral Activity

Postnatal development of cerebral activity recapitulates in the lifetime of the individual the development of mechanisms which have evolved genetically. At birth the cerebral cortex is like a blank book. When the baby's eyes have opened the nerves between the eyes and occipital lobes are not mature. The intake of stimulation is generalized and massive. Reactions to visual stimuli seem unrelated or unconnected to the stimuli. It appears that visual stimuli of various orders case the maturation of the visual cortex and the development of its responses from the general to the specific.

Man senses and feels only via the cells of the cerebral cortex. We may observe reflex actions in lower level reflexes, i.e., a burn does not elicit "pain" and pressure does not cause a "feeling of pressure." Thus, it may be said that perception (that which is affected by set and experience) is mediated only by the cerebral cortex in the intact organism. This contrasts with lower level or impaired organisms. The behavior of these organisms is integrated by lower level chemical and neurological mechanisms while, in higher organisms, all the concurrent actions of these lower mechanisms are integrated by the cerebral cortex. We find, therefore, that the lowest levels of the central nervous system are the most specific in function and the highest levels are the least specific. Man has no awareness of sensations coming from these lower centers. Many studies demonstrate that there is little spontaneous cortical discharge in the absence of afferent impulses. Unless there is an ongoing input of stimuli to the cortex, the level of cortical activity is diminished or absent; the cortex becomes less and less receptive to sensory experiences.

Cajal demonstrated that mylenization, at gestation, is well advanced in the primary cortex and in primary sensory projection areas of vision, touch, and hearing. It levels off and is absent in the parietal, occipital, and frontal lobes. Cajal also showed that the width of the entire cerebral cortex and each horizontal layer and the development of neurofibrils are affected by stimulus and response interaction. The growth, size, compactness of these structures, and the length of the process of the nerve are all involved in this interaction.

Grinker, to correlate with Cajal's findings, found that electrical potentials are comparable to those observed in the adult during sleep and are obtainable from the head of the human fetus at about the seventh month in utero (1951). At birth almost nothing identifiable as an E.E.G. is obtainable, but rhythmic fluctuations in potential will appear as soon as three months after birth. Thus, the way is prepared for cerebral integration and the reception of sensory information.

The Nerve

Thus far, we have dealt mainly with the structural elements of behavior. We can turn now to the activity processes of the nervous system, all of which bear on the educative, psychological, and rehabilitative processes.

The nerve (nucleus, axon, dendrite, etc.) can be seen from the viewpoint of its function as well as its structure. In this sense, the nerve acts as a "relay," with essentially two states of activity: firing and repose. Almost all neurons have messages fed into them by other neurons at points of contact known as *synapses*. Exceptions to these are those neurons that accept messages from free nerve endings or sensory organs and those where messages are initiated by energy factors: chemical or vibratory changes and physical phenomenon (light, heat, etc.).

The state of the incoming impulses at these synapses, combined with the antecedent state of the axon and its transmitter substances, determines whether or not a nerve will fire.

Every nerve, after firing at a given intensity of stimulation, has an absolute refractory state and a partial refractory state. Prior to recovery, a neuron can sometimes be in a state where it is neither firing nor refractory. When a number of incoming synapses fire (within certain, very short "fusion" intervals) and their cumulative energy exceeds a liminal threshhold, a neuron will fire. The intervening synaptic delay is fairly constant (Wiener, 1955).

The reception of stimuli is organized by a rather complex process. Only particular combinations of impulses from those incoming neurons that have synaptic connections with the given neuron will cause it to fire. Other combinations will fail to do so.

Action Potential

Another way of viewing nerve function is that of the *action potential*. A nerve impulse may be provisionally defined as a wave of electrical-chemical action that travels, without decrement, along nerve fibers. Eccles (1953) states that all "information" is conveyed via nervous impulses. More recent studies demonstrate an integral relationship between chemical and nerve mechanisms in this information process. To carry these analogies further, both nerve and muscle fibers may be regarded as cylinders of uniform diameter, extended indefinitely, and filled with a water medium of special composition (neuroplasm or myoplasm) (Haldane, 1947). These fibers are bathed in an internal solution that is an ultrafiltrate of blood, although different from it in composition.

The fibers are separated from the external medium (in vitro) by an exceedingly thin membrane. This plasma membrane is lipoid-protein in structure and has special electrical properties. These offer very high resistance to the diffusion of substances, especially ions (Eccles, 1953). The presence of an action potential, or subliminal firing, can be explained by a cycle of permeability changes at any region of this membrane. At this point, a small quantity of sodium ions is passed through the membrane, while a small quantity of potassium ions is pulled out. This action provides the immediate source of energy for the propagation of the impulse (Gellhorn, 1953).

This conducting core of nerve or muscle fiber also has the properties of a cable, since it is separated from the external conducting medium by the resistance of its surface medium. And, like a cable, if a steady potential change is produced at some transverse zone of the fiber—by the application of current or a chemical change—there will be a distribution of that current along the entire length of the fiber.

According to the ionic hypothesis, the action potential of the nerve impulse (spike) is generated by the influx of sodium ions that occurs when the membrane suddenly becomes highly and selectively permeable to them. The threshhold of the membrane is defined by that potential of depolarization at which the ingoing sodium current exceeds the outgoing potassium and chlorine current. This event initiates a self-regenerative action (Eccles, 1953).

The sodium-potassium exchange is enhanced by activity. Also, the functional effectiveness of the synapse is increased by activity.

Organisms, therefore, can be viewed as conglomerates of independent elementary units that untie and coordinate at certain levels (Jeffress, 1951). These units, in effect, are electrical/chemical organs. The stimulation of a neuron, the propagation and movement of its impulse, and the stimulating effects of the impulse at a synapse—all of these can be described chemically and/or physically.

As we said before, the neuron acts as an elecrical component and can be viewed as a switching or relay organ, a "black box." This "black box" responds to a specific stimulus or unity of stimuli by an energy response independent of the force of the stimuli (Ibid.). The energy output from a "black box," therefore, can be greater or less than the enegy input, producing *excitation* or *inhibition,* respectively. To illustrate this, imagine a burning fuse. The energy output here is at a given level. When it reaches the dynamite, however, that energy level determines neither the quantity of energy released nor the severity of the explosion.

In this manner the energy level of a nerve striking a ganglia or the central nervous system does not determine the level of energy released when the impulse is actually transmitted. A tiny impulse, acting as a "black box," can excite or inhibit large areas of the neural, humoral, and central nervous system.

To the educator, therefore, activity is seen as vital to the emergence of this process. Since amounts of activity and change do not themselves determine the *total* energy output of the nerve cells, we may hypothesize that *any increase in activity and stimulation* is rewarded by greater levels of firing. This achieves higher and higher levels of stimulation with subsequent increases in mentation or inhibition. Here many brain centers perform the function of a "black box." Clinically, we have often found the individual response of a client after a program of activity to be of a higher order than previously seen.

The Integration of Nervous Activity

Messages passing along the fiber are really a series of impulses. They travel at speeds ranging from approximately 250 miles per hour to less than 60 miles an hour. Each impulse is accompanied by a small electrical disturbance equivalent to about one-twentieth of a volt. And each nervous impulse is as powerful as the fiber is able to carry. We can see, then, that different kinds of impulses are not carried in one fiber, but that impulses are differentiated by the character of the individual fiber. And the effect of an impulse depends mainly on the connections of the fiber, not on the quality of the impulse (Haldane, 1947).

Without reservation, all nervous activity is reflex activity. A reflex is a reaction of an organism to the internal or external environment and is effected through the nervous system (Pavlov, 1928). All stimulation flows through the *foci* of brain we call *receptor centers*. These centers analyze everything in the central nervous system. Motor regions of the cerebral hemisphere are foci of receptor centers. In the same manner, the occipital region serves the eye and the temporal region serves the ear.

Pavlov demonstrated the relationship of these foci to behavior. He destroyed (ablated) variant cerebral centers and found an absence of true paralysis. By stimulating motor receptor foci, movement of a given limb or organ was elicited. Experimental animals, when the ablation of cortical areas is completed and they are free from narcosis, begin to make movements of all the extremities. Although there is damage to cerebral centers, all the muscles are in activity and not a single one is paralyzed. The subcortical centers continue to operate reflexively, often independent of the influence of external events. Function is affected, however: disturbances in coordination and movement can be seen.

Movements in higher animals do not exist preformed (i.e., when the animal is born). Rather, movements are elaborated by practice (learned). Those reactions we call conditioned motor reflexes are movements which are gradually formed by integrating unconditioned reflexes and lower behavioral centers. This process forms pathways in the brain throughout the life of the individual. Consequently, the sudden loss of a large mass of external stimulation, by which means movement is realized, results in the animal's inability to make any specialized movements. If Faradic stimulation is applied to the neuromuscular mechanisms, however, they will prove to be intact.

When we use postural or stretch reflex mechanisms at the Institutes we also elicit reflex motor activities and patterns. This occurs in the absence of cortical integration. When we discuss the elements of facilitation of neural discharge and its effects on cortical activity and on receptor foci, we can integrate the functioning of the receptor foci into a concept of learning.

It should be mentioned here, however, that the conditioned reflexes are contained in the highest part of the central nervous system. Here, there is a constant collision of innumerable influences from the external world. Among the different conditioned reflexes, there is an incessant battle at any given movement for a choice among them. Hull confirms this viewpoint with his concept of the behavior network and the levels of integration. He stated that a stimulus, with its intensity, trace experiences, function, and connections, is received in relation to a hierarchy of values. Each event, in turn, elicits those trace elements stored from past events.

When a physical therapist performs manual muscle testing, what is usually being examined is the cerebral nerve-muscle connection system. Our experience at the Institutes had demonstrated, however, that subcortical nerve-muscle reflexes can be elicited in the absence of those connections when we elicit lower level reflexes involving the muscles. This demonstrates the presence of a behavior network below the cortical level. We suggest that a system of manual muscle testing to ascertain the strength of the subcortical connections be developed. This would provide additional information on neuromuscular processes and prove valuable to programs of therapeutic exercise to enlarge and develop new levels of cortical connections. (See Appendix B.)

Inhibition and Habituation

Pavlov calls the breaking down of the conditioned responses "inhibition." Inhibition seems to be the tendency for conditioned responses to return to their unconditioned primal states. Accordingly, a conditioned reflex will be weakened, or inhibited, if the repeated application of a conditioned stimulus is not reinforced (habituation). In addition to this concept, Pavlov states that a continued repetition of stimulus (or constant environmental stimulus, C.E.S.) tends to lose its effectiveness unless the original stimulus is brightened and intensified. Under normal conditions, cortical activity soon becomes exhausted with repeated stimuli. This results in a state of habituation.

The implications of these findings urge the educator to evaluate factors of frequency and intensity of a stimulus in a learning situation. For example, talk that is not modulated can lead to habituation. Visual cues and the environment, unless varied, can be factors in inhibition; such constancy (C.E.S.) can also lead to habituation. Under these conditions, attention is lost and learning ability drops.

It must also be noted that cells recover during inhibition. They are inactive during this state and low intensity stimuli becomes effective once more. However, continued use or activity can lead to exhaustion. Initially this may be localized, but if allowed to continue the effect will spread. Thus, exhaustion becomes a form of inhibition.

Sleep occurs when irradiation from inhibitory regions (especially from thalamic areas) or pathways spreads over the entire cortex and some of the lower portions of the brain. Excitation, on the other hand, at a level of intensity (V) prevents inhibition *(threshhold liminal (*SLR)*). When stimulation originates in the hemispheres, it then spreads and irradiates over the cerebrum (Ibid.). The irradiated excitation gathers along certain paths and towards certain foci (Ibid.). This process, correlated with a psychological event, causes what is called the *Spread of Effect*.

Irradiation of stimulation to the subcortical centers can be clinically observed, however. When, as in a stroke, higher levels of integration are affected, an action such as a yawn can result in the raising of an arm or leg. In cerebral palsied patients, activating the ball of the foot by pressure, standing, or using the reflex hammer can elicit postural and myotatic tension. A flaccid encephalitis victim demonstrates tonic reflexes when his head is turned or pulled back.

The higher parts of the brain in the intact organism inhibit reflexes which the lower areas otherwise would carry out. These higher centers also mediate and control lower level reflexes, and can either include them in a process or effect movement without utilizing them at all.

We can see, from all these factors, that an impulse does not cross every synapse it comes to. Consequently, one impulse is capable of cancelling out the effect of another. This is yet another mechanism of inhibition. Thus, conflicting instructions or experiences can lead to inhibition of learning or performance, allowing for another system to be elicited.

Mind and Electrical Brain Factors

There is generalized agreement that all afferent volleys to the cerebral cortex generate an initial, surface positive wave therein. This is restricted to the cortical region in which the volley terminates (Eccles, 1953). Only when there is a high level of this activity in the cerebral cortex is liaison with the mind possible. This can be revealed by an E.E.G. This test also shows that the cortex may be at rest or it may be active only in a low degree or in a driven, stereotypic way (as in convulsive epilepsy or shock therapy). As such, the neuronal net is not in contact with the mind. When liaison does occur, The E.E.G. shows specific patterns of activity (Ibid.).

Fulton (1951) presents evidence to show that when the rate of stimulation in nearly any excitable focus of the central nervous system (CNS) is changed, the character of the response will be altered. Either excitation or inhibition can be obained by altering the rate of stimulation (Ibid.). When higher centers have been ablated, many activities of lower segments are eventually released. They can be more readily utilized then and observed in learning and activity situations (Deny-Brown, 1929). In contrast, integration in the intact organism proceeds down from the cortex.

Message Theory

Neurons and sense organs deliver a message of repeated, brief, electrical impulses called spikes. These are all equal in size but they increase in frequency when the stimulus is made more intense. Thus the message in the individual nerve fiber has the character of a simple frequency code. This code diminishes in frequency during continuous stimulation.

The sense organs are our private "measuring instruments." As with other instruments, they have properties such as sensitivity, range, speed, and power of resolution. It is these qualities that give rise or origin to the spikes (messages).

Rarely, if ever, are sensations based on the frequency code of one single afferent stimuli. Rather, sensation originates from many-fibered patterns, which are transformed or modulated on their way to the final receiving centers of the brain. Thirty percent of all the sensory input man receives is delivered through his one million optic nerve fibers (Fulton, 1951).

Feedback

An extremely important factor in voluntary activity is what control engineers term "feedback." For example, we may initially want a motion to follow a certain pattern, but the motion actually performed may be different from the one desired. This difference is noted and used as new input to cause the specific part to move in a manner closer and closer to the pattern originally desired. Each unit of new input, therefore, is "feedback."

The same process occurs when we attempt to pick up a fork. A report, conscious or unconscious, is sent to the CNS relating each time we attempted to pick up the fork and by what amount we failed. If we can see the fork, the report will be visual as well as the more general kinesthetic, tactile, and proprioceptive messages.

Defective feedback occurs when one of the necessary senses, such as the proprioceptive, is wanting and we have not replaced or substituted another sensation (tactile, kinesthetic, etc.). The total message received will be incomplete and innaccurate and we will be unable to pick up the fork. This leaves us, in this case, in a state of ataxia.

Excessive feedback is likely to be as serious a handicap as defective feedback to organized activity. An "intention tremor," for example is associated with injury to the cerebellum and is a consequence of excessive feedback (Wiener, 1951).

In many mental retardates the slow movements, backward pointing, and intention tremors indicate factors of possible cerebral pathology.

Some of this ataxic activity is correctble by therapeutic exercise and activity. Rather than strengthening the muscles, as we do in cases of paresis, we stress coordination, rhythm, balance, and timing. Using the former method is a common error in rehabilitation and nets poor results in alleviating the ataxic condition. Many of our patients were thought to be paretic rather than ataxic and, unfortunately, were treated as such.

Current studies gives us a rationale for the employment of our techniques, such as rail-walking, rather than the traditional muscle-strengthening exercise programs, to correct ataxic imbalances and mediate intention tremors. It has been shown that the central nervous system is not a self-contained organ, receiving input from the sense organs and discharging it into muscles. Rather, some of the most characteristic activities of the CNS are explicable only when seen as circular processes: input emerging from the nervous system into the muscles and reentering the nervous system through the sense organs, whether by proprioception or the more specialized senses.

In addition, many of the techniques used in therapeutic exercise for ataxic, cerebral palsied, and stroke patients may be employed profitably with individuals having more diffuse organic brain maldevelopment and malfunction. Although these latter malfunctions seem most often to be subclinical, the collective effect of these pathologies is clinical. They can be seen as part of the syndromes of subnormality and dysfunction: retardation, ataxic cerebral palsy, and learning disablties are common examples.

Feedback, therefore, represents an important source of information. Mechanisms elicited by pressure, pain, sound, taste, vibration, chemical changes, etc., send messages which are eventually integrated and coordinated by their particular neurohumoral systems. These different bits of information are unified, finally, in the higher centers and elicit the more coordinated and enlarged sensations of objects, conditions, and situations.

Learning

Hinde (1970) and others have stated that we are born with basic data and that all the information an organism obtains in its lifetime is accumulated on a foundation of innate releasor mechanisms (IRM's). Weiner's approach to learning states that the brain has all the data about the external environment inserted into it during life. According to his theory, data, and the means of combining that data, are learned. We can extend these concepts into the educational and clinical areas. Using growth, development, and experiences of the IRM's as a background, we can insert data via all the sensory pathways to modify behavior. With this approach as a guide, the techniques of counseling, teaching, and therapy will use the physiological information as a foundation to change behavior and not as an excuse for accepting the behavior first encountered.

Memory

Memory is the storage of information and its recall in new situations. As we mentioned before, memory can be either short term (stm) or long term (ltm). The condenser (Ibid.) is one of the simplest methods of storing information for a relatively short time, then discharging it under certain conditions. Long term storage of information requires a permanent alteration of certain storage elements, as in photography, for example. The neurons and synapses of the nervous system are storage elements of this sort. It is quite plausible that information is stored over long periods of time by changes in the threshholds of neurons, i.e., by changes in the permeability of each synapse to messages (Ibid.).

Reinserting information into this storage system will necessarily cause changes that bring about a discharge of the stored information. This process, in turn, affects the new messages passing through the system. As charged particles, these traces of earlier information now affect the manner in which all new information is transported through the system.

Cortical Tonicity and Integration

In many people who suffer the loss of a hemisphere of the brain, with a nearly complete loss of cortex, we have found the mutilated side is by no means dead. Voltages quite large can be observed to arise in the side where the cerebral cortex is gone, but the spontaneous activity—unstimulated rhythmic activity—is always attenuated considerably on that side. The ablated side cannot be stimulated nor messages elicited and, since the preservation of message information is dependent on the cerebral cortex, it is no longer a basis for integration of the subcortical systems.

Sherington (1948) states that an incoming afferent impulse may eventually produce at a given efferent neuron either a *central excitory state* (C.E.S.) or a *central inhibitory state* (C.I.S.). Just as a certain amount of depolarization is necessary for a nerve fiber to discharge, it is postulated that here a certain amount of threshhold excitation is necessary for the discharge of neurons. Also, any impulses that tend to depress a neuron will cause a central inhibitory state (C.I.S.). A neuron will discharge impulses when its C.E.S. has been raised to threshhold strength. It will continue to do so until the C.E.S. again drops below that threshhold strength. An incoming impulse will then repeat the process, producing a C.E.S. and inducing the cortex to activity.

Experiments have been done to study the effects just discussed. In one of these studies, the cortices of cats were treated as an isolated organ. A slab of tissue—a layer of brain composed of grey matter with some of the underlying cortical fibers—was isolated from either the central nervous system or the adjacent cortex. The blood supply remained as the only connection with the animal. Results showed a complete lack of electrical activity in the isolated cortices, demonstrating the absence of massed spontaneous activity.

These cells were not dead, however; despite their inactivity, a single stimulus applied through surface electrodes produced a localized response. The tissue beneath the electrodes became negative to the rest of the brain. These responses were not altered by isolation. Repetitive stimulation produced an after-discharge in the same manner as the intact cerebral cortex.

"Prepotentials" which occasionally fail to propagate are observed in many preparations. They then form small, monophasic spikes of discrete, "quantal" sizes. Such abortive spikes are wiped out by antidromic bombardment of the spindles and by a moderate stretch. This gives rise to a regular series of full-size afferent impulses. The presence of steplike prepotentials and abortive spikes indicates that there are local obstacles which delay and, occasionally, block the propagation of "newborn" impulses after they have arisen at the receptor terminals. These experiments demonstrate that stimuli are essential to the functioning of the integrated system.

An example of the results just discussed is Katz's study of the eyes. Visual stimulation of the eyes gives rise to electropotentials in the optic nerve. Stretching of the muscle produces a depolarization of the sensory nerve endings. This depolarization spreads along the axons electrochemically and varies with the rate and amplitude of the mechanical stimulus. A resting spindle, therefore, is always in readiness for firing (Katz, 1950).

Studies on the functioning of an integrated system have developed the "membrane theory." This assumes that the nerve fiber acts like a cable, capable of conducting on the inside (core) and the outside. These two sides are separated by a membrane having the electrical properties of resistance and capacity. The application of an outside current "charges" the membrane until the threshhold of the nerve has been reached. At this point, the stimulus becomes effective and a spike potential is released. This creates a small, local current that discharges each adjacent area in turn.

Thus the wave or negative spike reaches potential along the course of the fiber. The application of the subliminal strength of current may charge the membrane adjacent to the electrode and produce an electrotonic potential (electrotonus). Any active region of tissue is relatively negative to an inactive region.

Brain Wave Variations

Alpha rhythm frequency bands are between eight and thirteen cycles per second, and they possess a size or amplitude of about thirty-millionths of a volt. Neither the frequency nor the amplitude is constant. Each individual has his own characteristic pattern of frequencies and sizes. Thus each person's brain has a "print" that is as distinctive as his fingerprints.

Alpha rhythms can be identified by the part of the brain from which they originate. They are nearly always largest at the back of the head, where nerve signals from the eyes reach the brain. Alpha rhythms are usually larger and more regular when the eyes are closed and the person is not thinking.

Communication, therefore, between the projection and cognition areas must occur by a scanning mechanism. It would seem that the potentials of the human brain are inexhaustible. But, if we were unable to communicate with the world around us, how would we obtain the input of needed information for storage? A man robbed of his senses is like a recording machine with a fixed tape. Without input and connections to the C.E.S. and C.I.S., the brain, like the tape, could not play back and affect behavior.

Consciousness

All the activities of the cerebral cortex, including the incoming sensory impulses, the outgoing motor impulses, and the associations made within the cortex, constitute consciousness. In some way, sleep and anesthesia lessen or block completely the functioning of the cerebral cortex and produce unconsciousness.

Frequently, it has been suggested that some cells in the cortex can discharge spontaneously without being driven by afferent impulses. Burns studied a particular form of periodic, "spontaneous" neural activity. He created a focus or origin for this type of spontaneous activity by giving the central cortical surface a few strong electrical stimuli. This produced a series of discrete afterbursts, having all the properties of the surface-positive response to a single electrical stimulus. Investigating the factors which contributed to the formation of such a focus, he concluded that each discharge of the cells in the network which conducts surface-positive responses makes further spontaneous discharge more probable. This held true *whether the discharge was driven or spontaneous.*

Experiments using microelectrodes, however, have failed to reveal discharges of cells from within an isolated and unstimulated cortex. Rather, reactivity is due to different rates of recovery of the reacting membrane potential of the two cell ends. The deep ends of these neurons repolarize more slowly than do their superficial extremities. A few srong stimuli applied to the central cortical surface will produce a series of bursts of neural activity. This activity usually continues for several minutes after stimulation has ceased.

Consciousness, the state in which a person is aware of himself and his environment, depends on the complexity of his nervous organization. Its range varies among different individuals—between the intelligent and the retarded, the newborn and the adult. Also, different levels of consciousness can exist in the same person, depending on the degrees of stimulation and fatigue he is experiencing. This has been confirmed by E.E.G. tracings.

For example, a person whose eyes are closed may show well-developed alpha potentials of a frequency of eight to twelve cycles per second and an amplitude of fifty-millionths of a volt. When he is alert or shows greater attention to stimuli—from either internal or external conditions—he exhibits potentials of the beta type. These are smaller in amplitude and have greater frequency. Beta potentials are indicative of greater cortical excitation and result in a discharge less synchronous than those responsible for alpha potentials.

As a person becomes drowsy, an E.E.G. shows that alpha potentials become interrupted temporarily and their amplitudes diminished. A study of E.E.G. sleep records supports the interpretation of sleep as a state of physiological de-afferentation. Considerable evidence exists for the importance of muscle tone and the significance of proprioceptive impulses for the maintenance of wakefulness.

The cerebral cortex is the seat of consciousness. Sleep is a psychophysiological condition in which consciousness is abolished temporarily but can be brought back readily by appropriate stimulation. It is characterized by a general increase in the threshhold of stimulation. The intensity of sleep can be measured by the relative strength of stimulation needed to awaken a person.

Sleep is the result, at least partially, of the cessation or reduction of impulses impinging on the sensory cortex. Relaxation of the muscles reduces the stream of proprioceptive impulses that characterize the waking state. And hypnosis is the partial inhibition of the cortex, resulting in a semi- or subconscious state. Sensation, therefore, is a reaction that occurs only with consciousness and is dependent on the activity of the cerebral cortex.

Conclusion

Every living individual can benefit from some learning or educational procedure. The question remains whether this learning takes place at the physical level, the precognitive level, or whether it can reach the class-room level. We have found that some physical techniques can be adapted to the classroom situation. But traditionally the answer to this question has depended on economics and the amount of time expended. That is, how much improvement or output will we obtain in return for our investment?

At the Institutes, our approach is that if a motor ability does not evolve at an age-appropriate time (according to Spitz, Gesell, or a time-expectancy framework), we test to ascertain whether or not movement can be elicited reflexively. If this is so, we continue to use the reflexes as a form of exercise, strengthening motor connections until voluntary move-ment becomes possible. We continue the exercise until it becomes inte-gratd at the cortical level, where all voluntary action originates.

We have had successful experiences in hundreds of cases in initiating reflex movement where there had been no movement at all. And we have observed the subsequent emergence of cortically integrated voluntary movement.

To effect movement, some inhibition needs to be elicited. These inhibit-ory reflexes are strengthened in the same way that excitant reflexes are elicited. As all activity is an interplay between excitant and inhibitory systems, effective activity is not possible when one or the other system in in disuse.

When we observe a weakened motor activity and it has been demon-strated that a person can perform the movement voluntarily, we strive to strengthen, integrate, and coordinate all his motor abilities. If the indi-vidual cannot perform the action, we attempt to assist him until he can complete it alone. If this method does not work, we proceed to use reflex-ive methods to initiate subcortical activity. The integration of motor activity then begins to ascend from the reflexive (subcortical) to passive-assistive (using cortical activity) to assistive (using even more cortical activ-ity). At this point we can attempt to bring motor activity to its final stage—active and voluntarily initiated and carried through. This stage is the most advanced and utilizes cortical level activity throughout. And whenever, in the course of our treatment, we fail to progress in his hierarchy, we return to passive techniques. Again and again we will attempt to elicit reflexive activity—the most basic component of any further progress.

This procedure is in sharp contrast to that used in most physical medicine programs. There, therapists wait for an action to develop from the passive level, bypassing the reflexive level. The therapist will aid an action to completion by passive asssistance only if it first appears voluntar-ily. If, within a given time, this technique fails to elicit even the weakest level of activity, further attempts to stimulate action are abandoned.

This traditional procedure relies on cortical initiations of some action. It ignores Pavlov's findings on intact cortical, subcortical, and reflexive systems. It also fails to take into account the fact that neuromuscular and neuromotor connections are intact at subcortical levels—levels capable of strong elicitation even against resistance and gravity.

We have found, in contradiction to the above approach, that reflexive subcortical mechanisms can be elicited using special exercise techniques. Reflexive exercise will elicit the desired action if any subcortical mechanisms remain intact. We confirm this daily in our exercise programs. Through these, elicited actions are strengthened by repetition and rehearsal; often, voluntary movement is achieved. This demonstrates that cortical level connections have finally taken place.

The Dolman-Delcato methods are much in line with a use-disuse approach. They utilize passive patterns and active postural positions and crawling to strengthen undeveloped systems through repetition—patterning. This is a valid approach. However, Dolman-Delcato also bypasses the reflexive systems, as does traditional therapy. They do not use this basic system to strengthen connections, nerve centers, or subcortical and cortical areas.

We can elicit 10,000 actions by using reflexive methods, compared to the one action elicited by traditional techniques. We do not wait for the rare voluntary movement to appear so that we can strengthen it. Rather, we elicit the action reflexively and then strengthen it, using the more traditional elicitation techniques. By using subcortical mechanisms we increase a thousand-fold the possibility of cortical integration eventually occurring. Activity is more certain to occur, develop, and be maintained. This is an essential purpose of our programs.

CHAPTER VI

The Basic Receiving Systems
And the Modalities of Response
(With Maryanne P. Toomey, M.S.)

The basic mechanisms needed for the initial survival of the individual are essentially biochemical and biophysical. The severely and profoundly handicapped exhibit a malgenesis or agenesis of at least one, if not several, of the mechanisms needed for independent living.

A developmental disability involves one or more of the modalities concerned with information. A handicapped individual may have an impaired ability to receive, record, or integrate input from the environment; or the person may lack the ability to utilize such information to adjust to environmental changes. Thus, the developmentally disabled individual has an impaired ability to become aware of general or specific events and needs, and/or an inability to use this awareness to gratify those needs.

Piaget assumed that every child inherited the basic mechanisms for sensory/motor development. By merely eliciting these mechanisms the child, via assimilation and accommodation, gradually related to objects and the world. In the developmentally disabled child, however, one or more of these physical and cognitive mechanisms has failed to evolve along the expected sequence of development. These errors in development cause an obstruction or delay in the initial growth, elaboration, and integration of sensory/motor mechanisms. The readiness of reflexes to respond to environmental events in an organized and precise way at the critical time can also be delayed or impaired.

If, for example, a blockage or arrest occurs early in development, the first stage of generalized, mass activity will be arrested. From this point on, as specific environmental events occur, any further activities involving the integration and elaboration of the reflexes will also be affected. Arrested development can occur even during the fetal period.

What we will see first among some developmentally disabled, therefore, is a deficiency in responding to specific environmental stimuli and a relative lack of sensory/motor exploration. The autistic, for example, often lack an initial sensitivity to changing stimuli and events. Superthreshhold stimuli are needed to elicit responses. And children who are motor-impaired and retarded are unable to respond as rapidly and frequently as normal children to startle sounds, changing lights, and other such events.

In the following section, we will discuss the effects of a developmental disability on mechanisms such as perception, orientation, and basic sensory systems that receive and act upon information and our philosophy, approach, and methods for treating these impairments. The activities described here are not all-encompassing but are those needed to achieve the threshhold level of stimulus—a just noticeable difference that will elicit an action. More advanced activities are described in other sections of this book.

At any level we are continually seeking methods for initiating a sensory or motor response and elaborating that response until it reaches a voluntary stage.

Perception

For an infant to reach the sensory-motor stage of development, he must first pass through a stage of integration of his basic information mechanisms. Input regarding the internal and external environment is received and is then connected to some kind of response mechanism. These operations are what we call "perception."

An infant utilizes a basic range of modalities via the perceptive mechanisms that are needed for exploration. From psychophysiological studies, it is apparent that all IRM's are initially associated in a weak manner with the integrative mechanisms—the PNS and CNS (peripheral and central nervous systems). Eliciting a reflex, whether motor or sensory, results in a sequential strengthening of function, integration, and swiftness of action. Thus, use itself affects subsequent events. In the developmentally handicapped, we have found that delayed or absent IRM's can be elicited at other times and that events that failed to occur earlier in life, or at some normally expected time, can still occur. Mechanisms apparently absent now seem to be elicited more often after attempts to do so have been continuous, often lasting many years. This is the reason for our supporting an active intervention program for all disability, and why we keep activating over a lifetime.

Basic Orientation

Basic orientation is the perceptive modality by which we locate ourselves in space. This is further elaborated by fixing an awareness of the body's location relative to the head and then, more totally, by fixing awareness of the body's location in space. The sensory mechanism involved in this operation is the vestibular nerve; it senses feelings of acceleration and changes in direction. This modality elicits entire sequences of torso positions and head, leg, and arm movements in response to stimuli.

We can elicit reflexes and responses related to basic orientation by a number of activities:

1. *Rocking:*
   a. Rocking Chair —   to experience forward and backwards motion, from a sitting position.
   b. Rocking Board —   to experience lateral, side-to-side rocking, also from a sitting position.
   c. Tilt Board —   used for both forward and backward and side-to-side rocking

2. *Feeling of Falling.* We elicit this to develop protective arm movements, and hand and leg movements related to balance.

3. *Hanging Upside-Down on Ropes.* This elicits protective mechanisms and furthers development of equilibrium.

4. *Tumbling in Different Directions.* This is done while the body is contained in a large, doughnut-shaped knot.

5. *Positions in Water.* This allows one to experience the head in a different quality of environment and space.

Other activities should allow for movement in different directions, changes of speed, and contrasts between moving and stopping. Some of the movements these activities should involve are:

1. Riding up and down on a seesaw; climbing up and down a flight of stairs; using a roller coaster device.

2. Stepping and riding in both a forward and backward direction.

3. Moving swiftly (self-propelled).

4. Running in a certain direction; changing direction at command; marking time.

Auditory

The sensory modality for hearing is, of course, the ear. It is a vibratory, mechanical sense organ.

We stimulate the ear by using various mild types of vibratory devices. We also stimulate the region of the ear and the bones surrounding it. We have noticed, on a number of occasions, an initial response to sound concurrent with or just subsequent to the use of this type of stimulation.

We also work on developing amplitude, or loudness. We use a number of amplifiers and various types of ear phones. Always starting the device at zero volume, we continue amplifying until we observe an initial generalized body response or a movement of the head or eyes. Frequently, children not known to respond to standard auditory tests were first observed to respond to this technique.

> Walter, whom we mentioned before, was first seen to be hyperactive, deaf, visually impaired, and autistic. He was an untestable youngster. Using the above techniques and others related to the visual area, Walter was behavior-modified. We were able to train him to listen and, finally, to respond to various initial voice commands.

We use these techniques for a period of time every day. Once any initial response has been observed, we play tapes for ten to fifteen minutes over the course of a month or so. Following this, we amplify initial commands over the same receiving system (amplifiers and earphones). Usually a drop in the *jnd* (just noticeable difference) threshhold occurs and a response can be elicited.

We feel the above experiences demonstrate that the initial connections are weak and the systems not integrated. With use, however, they become more efficient and the intensity of sound needed for a response becomes less and less.

Once we receive some response to sound, we attempt to remove the electrical systems and obtain a response to environmental sounds, or we attempt to get initial corrective hearing devices for the client. We try to initiate head turning and eye movement in response to environmental sounds and, ultimately, for locating sound sources in space. This operation utilizes visual scanning as a reflex response to sounds coming from a distance. We have seen both initial startle reflexes and the more advanced scanning reflex occur in older children in whom these had never been observed to occur.

We are also able to obtain a differential response by modulating the pitch of sound for each earphone separately. Eventually, this enables the child to receive and screen two different levels of sound at the same time, enabling him to obtain a more sensitive reception to different sound ranges.

We also introduce other sound qualities using these methods. The concept of "time" is experienced by sending sounds at different intervals. By varying the quality and pitch, we can introduce "tone" differences. We change the context of the situation for both experiences, thus broadening the range of stimulation and response.

Our twenty years of clinical work in this area raises an important question: namely, if, at some earlier stage, a response occurred at some level of intensity but was not subsequently associated to events, could habituation, a form of inhibition, have begun to take place?

Such conditioning would prevent these individuals from responding to the usual auditory test situations. Only an extended exposure to sounds at an intense, superthreshhold level would elicit a response. Under constant environmental conditions or after prolonged exposure to such constancy, individuals would be forced into relying only on internalized stimuli (autistic in quality), merely to maintain their survival. Consequently, such profoundly handicapped individuals would be unable to respond to traditional testing procedures, whether such testing is done for auditory or any other sensory modalities.

This is an issue that warrants further study and confirmation. From our years of experience, we can only assume the above to be true. Hence our intense and continuous attempts to initiate, or reinitiate and strengthen the releasor mechanisms—via the modulation of the environment and the intensification of stimuli to superthreshhold levels.

Visual

We have been amazed by the number of children who initially appear to be profoundly retarded, nonambulatory, and unaware but whose primary problem is one of balance.

To remedy this situation, we attempt to initiate focus. We place goggles on the child and shield the sides of his face, thus narrowing the visual field. If we then observe an initial visual response to objects, we have an indication that we are dealing with a visual or occular-motor problem.

Following this procedure, we begin stimulation with a penlight to initiate eye movement. We continue this activity and gradually add other activities that stimulate and give the child experiences in the following areas:

1. Contour	5. Background	9. Azmuth
2. Shape	6. Brightness	(Direction)
3. Symmetry	7. Color	10. Texture
4. Foreground	8. Intensity	11. Depth

Such a program has enabled many of our children to show dramatic improvement that touched and mediated many areas of their functioning.

—Michael, aged three, was diagnosed cortically blind after a period of quasicoma. Shortly after being stimulated in the above fashion he was observed to be following his mother's face with his eyes. This was reported to his opthamologist, who proceeded to refract Michael's eyes and fit him with glasses. We then were able to begin a program of visual behavior with him.

—Walter, the deaf-blind child we mentioned earlier, was also treated in this manner. He, too, was able to wear glasses. He exhibited a whole new sequence of direct relations in his behavior, and his abilities at prevocational tasks ascended to the borderline-normal.

—Leslie and Suzey were able to focus and maintain sufficient balance for standing as a result of our program. They went on to programs for the blind and learning-disabled.

Olfactory (Odor-Nose)

Reaction to, or altered movement in response to common odors, such as food, are often diminished or absent in our children. We attempt to instigate alertness and reactivity to various olfactory events by first stimulating the various reactive modalities of the system:

1. Pungent (roses)
2. Irritant (ammonia)
3. Fragrant (flowers)
4. Putrid (rotting meat)

We watch for alerting, scanning, or evading responses in relation to the odors themselves or to the tastes related to the odors. For example, the smell of lemon will elicit a sour reaction, a pungent odor will cause a reaction of the nose and mouth, tongue licking, and rooting responses.

Gustatory (Eating System)

Many profoundly handicapped children have atrophied palates, gullets, cheeks, teeth, and throat muscles. Typically, they have been bottle-fed with a paplike substance, or they were placed on an incline, had their heads tilted back and, literally, had the food shovelled into their mouths. Consequently, for many of our children, it is difficult to know whether innate releasor mechanisms for sucking, chewing, rooting, licking, etc., were ever elicited or whether they simply disappeared from disuse.

Rapid feeding and placing the food so far back in the mouth, beyond the location on the tongue of the taste buds, fails both to utilize the modalities of smell and the sensations of taste. Also, since the food is usually liquid or pap, it does not require chewing or swallowing to any great degree. As a result, much of the gustatory apparatus falls into disuse or develops deficiencies.

In our work, we try to elicit the innate gustatory mechanisms: first, by presenting various foods at the anterior part of the mouth near the tongue, cheeks, and region of the teeth. We use foods with primary tastes, such as:

1. Sour—pickle, juice, lemon, etc.
2. Sweet—sugar, honey
3. Bitter—white radishes
4. Spicy—peppers
5. Fatty—butter, bacon
6. Oily—olive oil
7. Rancid—turned butter or milk
8. Salty—pretzels

We also vary the texture and introduce contrasts with the above foods.

Concurrent with attempts to elicit taste reactions, we attempt to stimulate movements of the tongue. This is done by placing the bits of food on the lips and at different locations at the entrance to the mouth to elicit tongue action. During this type of stimulation, a block to tongue protrusion inhibits unwanted reflexive extension of the tongue and assists in proper utilization of the tongue in licking and chewing.

Chewing is induced reflexly by pressing hard rubber nipples against the upper palate. The bottles contain liquids or small amounts of pap. Soft foods such as applesauce and pudding are pressed to the upper palate with a spoon. As the chewing reflex is elicited, some of the food is spilled or eased off into the mouth (either to the rear or along the anterior tongue). This frequently elicits the swallowing reflex.

We then feed from different directions, giving the child a small taste of the food. This generally elicits head turning or forward movement of the head in an attempt to reach the spoon. The child may also try to grasp the spoon with his lips. We use this procedure; we also attempt to have the child grasp or hold the spoon with his hand. When we have reached this point we can move on to more traditional ways to feed the child and, eventually, teach him to feed himself.

Thermal (Skin Receptors for Temperature; Hot and Cold)

The severe and profoundly handicapped often are kept in constant environments, such as provided by an institutional setting. The indoor temperature is rarely varied and they are usually well-swaddled when they are taken outdoors. As a result, the sensitivity to different weather conditions and the general sensitivity to hot and cold is impaired. In addition, since institutional food is rarely varied and often is served lukewarm of inadequately heated, the children show a deficiency in responding to cold foods and hot soups and drinks.

To increase the child's awareness of temperature we first set up experiences for hot and cold, ice and warmth, as elements in themselves. We then integrate this into the larger, concurrent experience of objects that have been warmed or frozen. Finally, we use warm, hot, and cold foods. This experience augments the child's involvement with his environment.

Pressure/Pain

The pressure/pain modality is located in the superficial layers of the deep skin and the tongue. It responds to levels of pressure, crushing, and injury.

To increase the effectiveness of this modality, we first elicit alerting and movement in response to light stroking, using the fingertips or a brush. We then apply pressure. Tickling or pressure applied to a body part such as the ear, eye, or nose causes reflexive activity and either a generalized movement or actual, aversive hand and/or leg movements will occur. By thus atempting to ward off the uncomfortable or painful pressure, the child's movements trigger IRM's—often for the first time. The response gradually grows stronger and stronger.

We also grasp the toe or the tip of the finger, ear, or nose and place it under stretch (traction) for an extended period (three to ten minutes). This elicits aversive movement to kick or ward off the hold. Again, the IRM's being triggered are often appearing for the first time. We continue to elicit and strengthen these movements as they utilize motor elements that can later be used in other activities. The same elements in an aversive arm movement, for example, can be used for holding or moving toward an object, rather than avoiding it.

The Haptic Sense

This modality involves sense organs for pressure found in the skin. They are affected by the angles translated at the joints and represent the abilit to know objects from direct touching, holding, and experiencing.

To develop this sense, which is often deficient in our children, we start with passive holding and utilization of group reflexes. For example, a teacher may place her fingers through a child's fist and have him grasp the fingers as he is pulled up and dangled a small distance above the floor.

Proprioception

Sense organs are found in the stretch receptors of the muscles; they sense where the body part is in relation to itself and the environment. (See the preceding section on "Basic Orientation").

Spatial Discrimination

This modality helps us to distinguish background and foreground. We experience the difference between these two qualities by hearing, seeing, and actually moving between objects. For instance, as very young children we begin by finding and handling small objects on a table. Then we start to crawl and walk toward objects. This activity enables us to experience and understand the place relationship of one object to another. We learn to know, from any one point, what is near or far, close or distant from us.

The Motor Area

From the moment of conception our innate mechanisms for perception, movement, integration, and the higher mental processes are evolving and interrelating concurrently. The mechanisms for respiration, digestion, elimination, vision, neurointegration, muscle movement, etc., are all inherited. A normal child possesses a range of innate releasor mechanisms (IRM's) that are activated at appropriate times when environmental events elicit them. For example, muscle contraction first occurs through ionic exchange. Later, muscles contract through neural control. Finally, they are integrated into a reflex system.

Reflexes for all basic motor activities (arm and leg movements, walking, creeping, crawling, swimming) and all the sensory modalities are present in basic form from birth. These begin to be activated almost immediately after birth and during the early weeks. Also present are the mechanisms for receiving stimuli and the means, through all the perceptive modalities, for integrating stimuli. The initial reflexes can be elicited long before they become related to their functional use.

Development, then, appears to be a sequence of growth guided along genetic lines. All these mechanisms become progressively more integrated and stronger as the child grows and becomes more and more active.

In the developmentally handicapped, however, one or more of the motor or sensory-motor mechanisms may be absent or in a condition of malfunction of dysfunction. When we treat such an individual we first test to ascertain whether reflexive movement can be elicited. If so, we use those reflexes as a form of exercise to strengthen motor connections until voluntary movement is possible.

We have also had much success in initiating reflex movement where movement was absent. We disagree with the Bobaths that early reflexes should be inhibited. Rather, it has been our experience that stronger movement results when early movement activity is elicited. This activity progresses until voluntary movement appears.

To summarize, we observe the motor activity in question. If voluntary movement is possible, we strive to strengthen, integrate, and coordinate all motor abilities. And if this is not the case, we utilize any or all of the procedures discussed in the previous chapter. We may find it necessary to begin with eliciting reflexes. Or we may start with passive-assistive techniques until the individual can complete more and more of the activity independently. We use gradually less assistance as the client is able to use more and more voluntary movement and initiate and complete the activity on his own. On whatever level we begin treatment, we attempt to strengthen reflexes and coordinate and integrate motor abilities to progressively higher levels of control.

We utilize range-of-motion exercises throughout the process to increase joint mobility. As the joint becomes more capable of greater range the action becomes stronger. This, in turn, recruits more of the neuromuscular mechanisms. When a joint is limited in range of motion, the action of the muscles becomes obstructed. By using R.O.M. techniques we enlarge and strengthen the effectiveness of the reflexes we elicit. This procedure works even with those individuals whose muscles contract isometrically during activity, that is, the muscles contract but the limb or part does not move. Through the use of our strengthening activities and R.O.M. techniques, we have been able to increase the level of integration for this individual and prevent or ameliorate many of the consequences of disuse.

CHAPTER VII

The Gootzeit Procedure
To Determine Whether or Not
To Use Traditional or Reflexive
Exercise Procedures

The *Gootzeit Procedure* is employed to determine whether or not to strengthen motor ability via traditional exercise techniques or to pursue a program of reflex-initiated movement and exercise. To do this, we first use test techniques such as the Kendle, Worthingham, or other similar muscle-testing procedures. These can pick up responses when Normal (N), Good (G), Fair (F), Poor (P) and Trace (T) levels of muscle strength indicate that there is an intact level of cortical connection. The following lists the grade levels of muscle strength:

(N)	Normal	—Against resistance
(G)	Good	—Against some resistance
(F)	Fair	—Against gravity
(P)	Poor	—Gravity eliminated
(T)	Trace	—Some tightening of muscle
(0)	Zero	—No noticeable trace

If we cannot elicit activity in the poor position, possible cortical weakness is indicated. We feel that our technique of testing for subcortical and reflexive integration is then warranted. This technique can also test for levels of strength at N,G,F,P,T or O, but only by using reflexive (subcortical) methods to elicit the action.

NECK EXTENSION

Procedure One

To determine neck extension against gravity, we observe whether or not a child can lift his head from a table or if he can raise his head when it is dangled over the edge of a table. If he does not demonstrate this ability, we try to elicit head raising reflexly. The child is placed in the prone position as we press the head downward. This puts his neck on stretch and will, if possible, elicit reflex head raising. *(See Fig.1a-1c.)*, p .

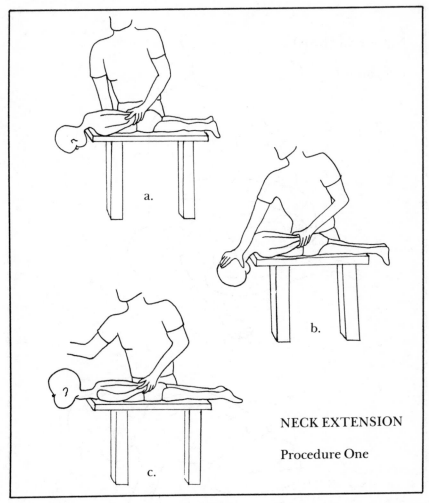

a.

b.

c.

NECK EXTENSION

Procedure One

Fig. 1

If the child does respond to this procedure, we pursue a strengthening system using stretch neck reflexes, traditional voluntary, and, then, resistive exercises.

Procedure Two

If the child cannot raise his head against gravity, we try to elicit neck and spinal extension in the Poor (P) Position, with gravity eliminated. Place the child in a sidelying posiion, knees to his head, and tickle or squeeze his nose. This elicits an evading action and resultant head and back extension. *(See Fig.2a-2b.)* p. .

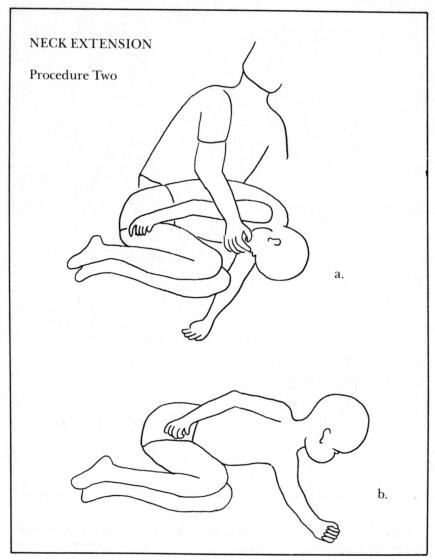

NECK EXTENSION

Procedure Two

a.

b.

Fig.2

Procedure Three

If the child cannot raise his head reflexly, we place him in the prone position and raise his head passively for ten repetitions, thus eliciting spinal reflex contractions all the way down to the heel cords. This strengthens subcortical systems by exercise and promotes eventual cortical integration of the now-enhanced system. *(See Fig.3)* p. .

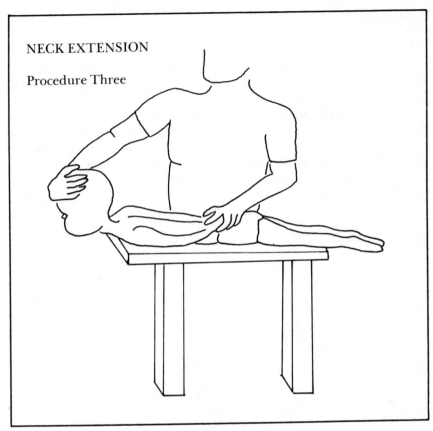

NECK EXTENSION

Procedure Three

Fig.3.

We build reflexive repetitions to fifty, with three or four trials per day to augment that ability. We continue this exercise until voluntary head lifting is observed. We can follow up this achievement with the next procedure, in order to increase the *frequency* of voluntary movement. We elicit this activity as part of a graduated repetitous program. As voluntary head raising increases, we first passively then actively strengthen activities again using repetition and exercise in the traditional manner.

Using the above rational for testing and exercise, we can proceed to test other subcortical, intact, neuromuscular mechanisms. We can utilize these reflexes for the muscles physiologically. In many instances, initial elicitation of reflexes leads to subcortical integration and to subsequent voluntary (cortical) action. This process can then be strengthened further, using traditional therapeutic exercise techniques via standard muscle-strengthening methods.

Abdominals

Procedure One

Lower Abdominals. Press the chin hard into the child's chest. This will result in abdominal contracting and, possibly, he will be able to raise his head and shoulders off the mat.

Upper Abdominals. Next, place the child in the supine position with his legs extended. Place the hand on the chest just below the sternum and press (Steady Press), then push the chin into the chest. The hip muscles will contract and the abdominals also. After some repetition, the legs may be raised, thus strengthening the abdominals and the reverse action of the hip flexors. If this fails, scratch or press the soles of the feet to elicit withdrawal reflexes. Lock the knees so that the legs come up straight. *(See Fig. 4a.-4b.)* p.

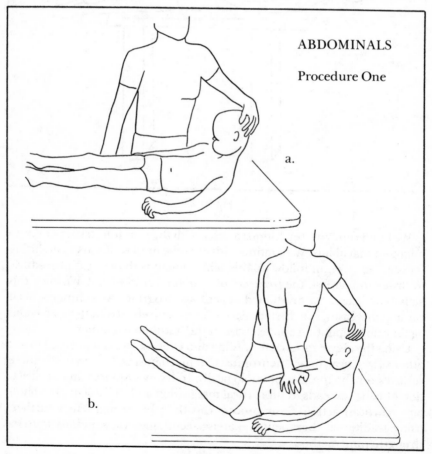

Fig. 4

Procedure Two

Lower Abdominals (gravity eliminated). Place the child in the supine position, hooklying, with his knees up. Then, press his chin to chest until he sits up. *(See Fig. 5a.-5b.)* p.

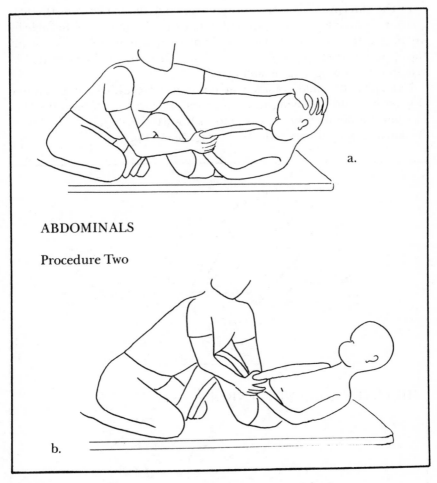

ABDOMINALS

Procedure Two

Fig. 5

We use the above procedures as exercises to strengthen subcortical integration of the motor system. The goal is the eventual cortical integration of abdominal action. If reflexes are absent, we use passive movement toward strengthening subcortical connections.

HIP FLEXION AND EXTENSION

When a child lacks hip flexion or extension, as indicated by traditional muscle-testing techniques, we proceed as follows:

Procedure A. Hip Flexion

In the sidelying, poor (P) position—gravity eliminated—set the legs apart in a walking posture. Flex and stabilize the leg that is off the table by holding it. If you obtain unilateral symmetrical action, stabilize or tie off the opposite arm and leg (for each action). This aides in the elicitation of reciprocal creeping motion later on.

Next, place the child in a sidelying position with the hip hyperextended. Rotate the head (sidelying tonic neck reflex) and stretch until the chin touches the shoulder or, at least, moves toward the shoulder. Hold until flexion at the hip occurs reflexly. (See Fig. 6a.-6b.) p.   .

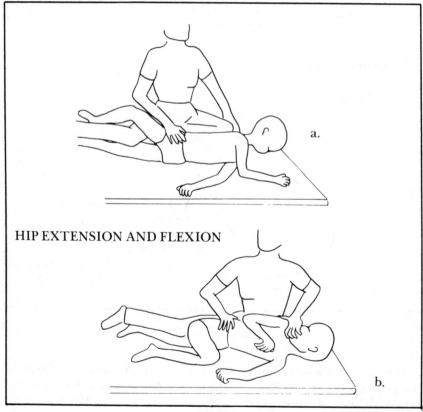

HIP EXTENSION AND FLEXION

Fig. 6

Procedure B. Hip Extension.

Keep the child in a sidelying position, hip flexed. Stabilize the upper leg by holding it. Rotate the head to the shoulder, as above, until hip extension is elicited reflexly. *Note:* Fig. 6 illustrates hip extension also, by examining the figure from "b" to "a" and using the procedure just described under "Hip Flexion." *(See Fig. 6b.-6a.)*

CREEPING

Procedure

Place the child flat in the prone, fencing, creeping position. With his head to one side, stretch the chin to a ninety-degree angle, then rotate the head to the opposite side and stretch. Observe for reflexive creeping actions of the arms and legs. They may be reciprocal (unilateral) or alternate (bilateral). The bilateral action is a higher reflex development. *(See Figs. 7, 8, 9.)*

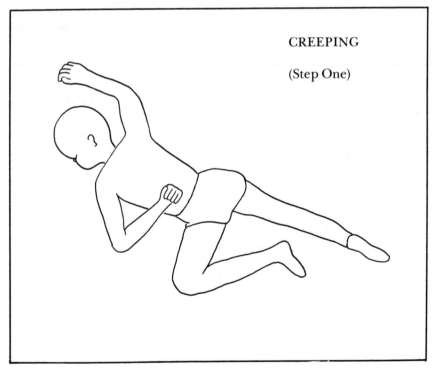

CREEPING

(Step One)

Fig. 7

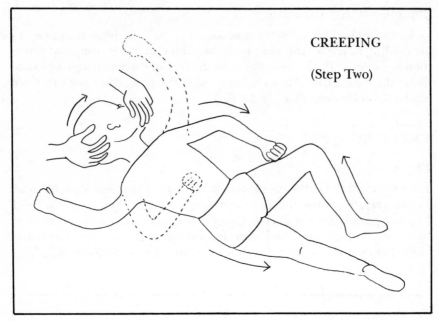

Fig. 8

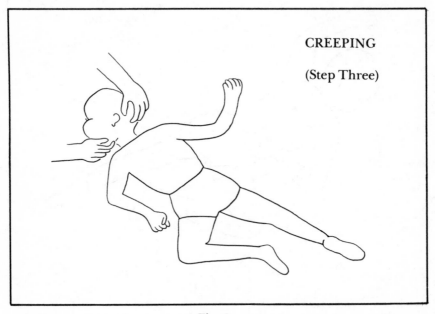

Fig. 9

CRAWLING

Procedure One

This is used to raise the child to all fours for the crawling position. Place the child prone, put his hands alongside his head, press his chin down into his chest. The child will rise to all fours if the reflex can be elicited. *(See Fig. 10a.-10b.)* p.   .

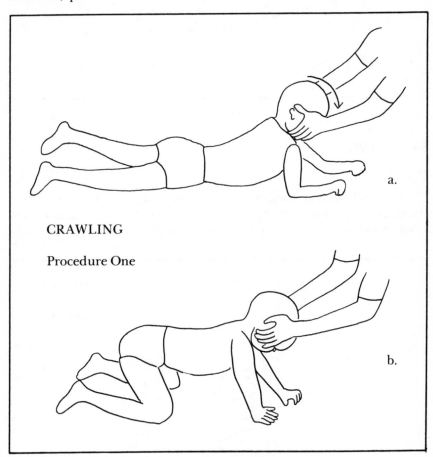

a.

CRAWLING

Procedure One

b.

Fig. 10 (a, b)

Procedure Two

If Procedure One does not elicit the crawl position, lift the child by his shoulders, let his head drop to stretch, and let his arms hang to the floor. *(See Fig. 10c.)* p.   .

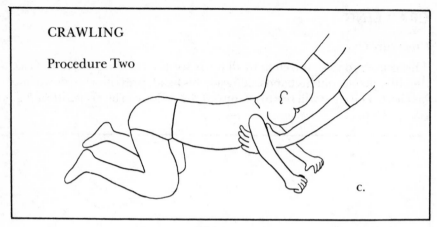

Fig. 10 (c)

STANDING

Procedure One

Place the child with his back to the wall. Hyperextend the knees and allow the child to straighten to a standing position. A swift hyperextension will result in an increased awareness, a startle-type of reflex. *(See Fig. 11.)* p.   .

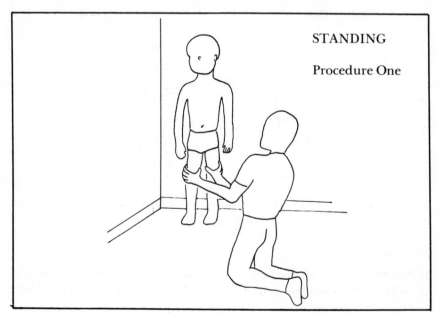

Fig. 11

Procedure Two

With his arms over the back of a chair or with some arm grips, cause the child to dangle his feet until he attempts to step (parachute). The standing reflex will be elicited, Further standing is done in a tilt board, to assist in joint action being immobilized and to prevent deformities in bones and joints because previous standing activity was absent. *(See Fig. 12.)* p.

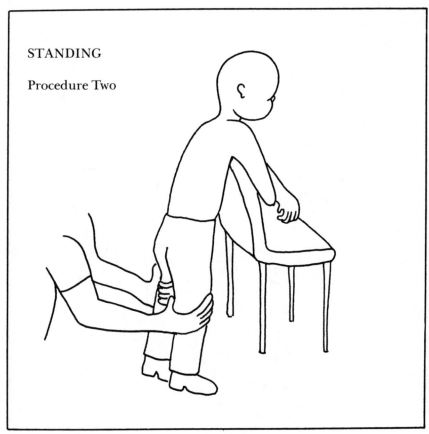

STANDING

Procedure Two

Fig. 12

Procedure Three

Lift the child under his arms, at the hips. He can then come to a standing position. There are a few other techniques for eliciting the standing action (arm grip, under arms, parachute, head hold.) *(See Fig. 13.)* p.   .

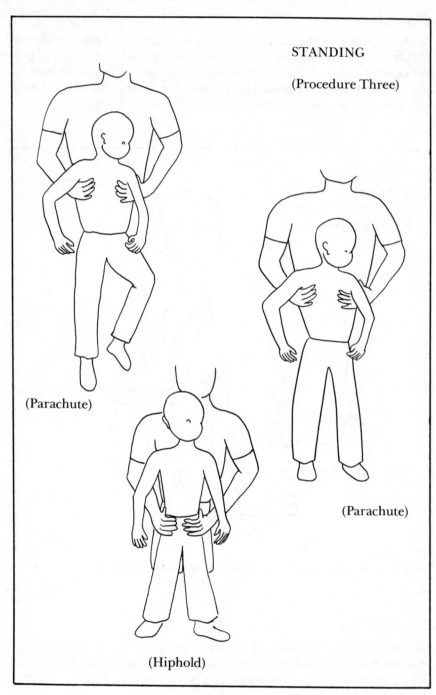

Fig. 13

WALKING

Procedure One

Walking can be elicited by grips or by use of a walker or chair, gradually pulling the child off balance. This elicits steps to recover footing. *(See Fig. 14.)* p. .

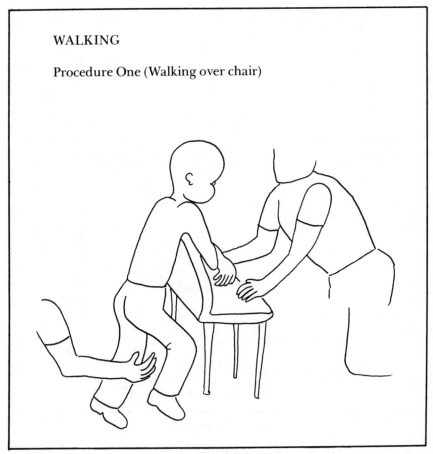

WALKING

Procedure One (Walking over chair)

Fig. 14

Procedures Two and Three

Other techniques can include arm holding, underarm or headhold and wrist and hand supination. *(See Fig. 15.)* p. .

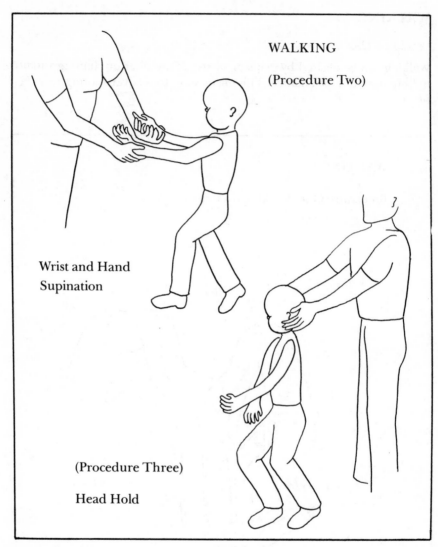

WALKING

(Procedure Two)

Wrist and Hand
Supination

(Procedure Three)

Head Hold

Fig. 15

HANDS, ARMS AND FOREARMS

Procedure

For reflexly strengthening (isometrically) arms and hands. Put the child over a bolster in order to force him to support himself on his arms. Since he will be off balance, he will then have to use his arms to keep himself from falling. This contracts the muscles of the chest, arms, forearms, and hands. *(See Fig. 16.)* p. .

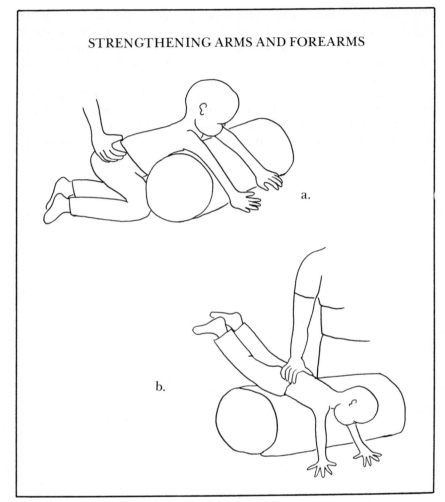

STRENGTHENING ARMS AND FOREARMS

a.

b.

Fig. 16

GRASP

We place blocks on the eyes to disturb vision, or we irritate the ear with a tiny hair brush, until the child brings his arms up to brush off the therapist's hand or block her movements. After a number of successful repetitions, as the child tries to grasp the therapist's fingers to force removal of the disturbing object, we place an object in his hand as he raises it. This causes an increment in object-holding and touch-exploration of other objects.

We have developed many more reflex procedures at the Institutes of Applied Human Dynamics. *(See Appendix B)*. To present all of them would make this book far too lengthy. And, much of what we actually do is an applied art, one that is better taught in therapeutic practice than with mere words.

We hope that, as others follow the principles of these techniques for each muscle group, unlisted and unchartered reflexes will be found and utilized to strengthen integration. We will thus add to our ability to prevent disuse, using reflex techniques to lead to the hoped-for voluntary actions.

CHAPTER VIII

The Higher Mental Processes

The next group of mechanisms relevant to the severe and profoundly handicapped are those involved in high level mental processes. Explorative behavior, comprehension, cognition, learning, perception, and problem solving: these are both stages and results of an individual's needs, his reactions to his environment, and his desire to survive and grow.

For the severely handicapped as well as for any individual to function on a higher level than the purely organic, it is essential that reception, integration, and reaction to stimuli take place in an increasingly complex and coordinated manner. Innate mechanisms receive and coordinate information to a system of effector mechanisms. The entire process occurs continuously and enables the individual to see, understand, and relate to the world around him.

In the following section we shall discuss the workings of such high level mental processes and the effects of severe handicaps on their effectiveness. We have found, during our years at the Institutes, that many profoundly handicapped individuals can achieve levels of awareness and capability once thought to be forever beyond their reach.

Exploration

The process of exploration begins in the presence of objects or events. At first, only the actual and immediate object or effect is experienced. Stimuli impinge directly on the organism or its distal receptors. Receptor mechanisms, formed and ready before birth, now begin to receive and process this basic information. Thus, a groundwork is built for future and more complex information; the individual begins to "know" his world.

The Neural Behavior Net (NBN)

The responsiveness to stimuli is modulated and differentiated by their relevance to an individual's needs. Comprehensive, need-related mechanisms are activated as different needs arise to seek a response. How strong the needs, whether they are crucial to survival or less important, whether they are basic or more advanced—all these factors determine which mechanism will be stimulated and which reponse will be given at any one time.

An individual will respond as a whole entity to each need. However, stimuli that corresponds to the uppermost needs at that time (for food, water, sex, intellectual processes) will be received at a lower threshhold than any other concurrent stimuli. For example, a person who has just finished a full meal might have a much stronger desire to take a walk or a nap than for more food. And only a superthreshhold stimulus, such as a favorite dessert, might tempt him to remain at the table. Similarly, the immediate need to survive will supercede all other needs: escaping from a burning building becomes more crucial than food, money or possessions.

Once initial explorative behavior helps the individual to learn about his world on a basic level, the innate releasor mechanisms relevant to simple objects and situations become integrated into a central integrating mechanism. This triggers mechanisms that begin to elicit the perceptive modalities. All of these coordinate and function to direct the individual to those events and objects that will satisfy his needs. A person thus begins to have more and more control and direction in his life.

For the severely handicapped, however, this process of learning and mastery is deficient. Some receiving or integrating system has failed to develop or is not functioning properly—seriously enough to curtail or make impossible the entire process. In our work, we return to very beginning stages of exploration. We present objects such as food or a toy directly. Once the object becomes desired, a condition of privation is established. The object is withheld for a certain period of time and, as the need increases, the threshhold for reception of stimuli from that object is lowered. The child begins to associate a specific object with a specific need. Following this, we present stimuli related to the object (the odor of food, a small bit of it placed on the lips or near the mouth). This sort of stimuli elicits movements to obtain the food or object, now that the child already knows it relates to his needs. He has begun to orient and direct his activity towards satisfying his particular desires. On a more advanced level, a child will begin to lick his tongue or turn his head just in anticipation of the desired object. This response to associated and anticipated objects or events demonstrates that an initial memory of what follows has been acquired. Image formation, essential to all learning, has occurred.

A child can now be given more advanced tasks related to the storage of images. An object known to the child is hidden and the child is asked to find it. We may then give him a seqence of tasks leading up to findng the desired object. For example, "Go to the kitchen"—"open the refrigerator," "get me the orange." If the child can move through such a sequence and obtain the object, in this case, the orange, he demonstrates that image formation and the storage of those images has been acquired.

Rehearsal and Recall

We have found that repetition of experience (rehearsal) seems to enhance and strengthen an individual's initial memory (recall) of an object or situation. This, in turn, creates a stronger foundation for the presentation and mastery of new objects and events.

In the course of this process, we have found it best to begin with discrimination tasks that require two steps to complete, or to differentiate between two objects. We repeat this procedure a number of times and on subsequent days (trials). As a child is successful with this level, we then add tasks requiring three steps, then four steps, and so on. Each level of accomplishment becomes gradually more complex and utilizes all the previously acquired successes.

Comprehension

As an individual's ability to remember objects and perform recall tasks develops, we try to determine if he is also able to use this skill to understand content and meaning. If so, he can be given more complex types of instructions, directions, and signals. Ultimately, this ability can be integrated into problem-solving activity.

Problem-Solving Activity

An individual engages in problem solving when he performs a sequence of activities to satisfy a particular need or to attain a desired solution. The process appears to be image-driven and related to experiences in solving more basic needs. From the modalities of exploration and perception an individual now has an increased ability to touch his environment, receive and process stimuli from internal and external sources, and connect all this information with response mechanisms.

Cognition

"Meaning" emerges from experience as image mechanisms process inherited and learned stores of information. A particular event or object will now elicit a "knowing" of that object or event. This is the process of cognition.

Learning and Perception

Learning is an elaboration of an individual's inherited tendancies to behave relative to events and situations that he experiences. And, by the process of perception, he gives recognition and meaning to those events.

Perception seems to be related to both experience and awareness; experience alone does not result in a percept. Only if the event, through various levels of an individual's awareness, is stored (memory) will perception occur.

Learning is achieved in terms of what is perceived. Without perception, events will not be remembered nor form new memory. If the storage or sensory mechanisms are faulty, or if the process itself is unbalanced and uncoordinated, the information will be recorded as distorted. Unless other perceptive mechanisms in the brain can help to correct this imbalance, the responses to such information will also be distorted and inappropriate.

The brain, with its cells and tissues, is also affected by use and disuse. Awareness is a function of the cerebral cortex; learning and perception consequently require large amounts of brain tissue for processing information. Any condition that lessens or destroys numbers of brain cells, therefore, would have direct effects on awareness, learning, and perception. Aging, for example, results in increased mortality of cerebral cells. Disuse of cerebral cortex mechanisms can also cause a shriveling and death of brain cells. Therefore, any study of learning and perception must regard retardation (human slowness) as a deficiency of the learning process-a deficiency related not to motivation but to developmental processes of the brain itself.

Awareness also brings to the cerebral cortex the kinesthetic sensations of various movements the body is performing and resident sensation from parts of the body at rest. It is essential for an individual to be able to focus attention and receive input from these sensations if he is to acquire control over different movements. As he refines and augments this ability, new nervous connections are formed and strengthened. The nervous system constantly integrates and modifies reflex center activity as new learning takes place.

The neurobehavioral organs of control are very malleable. Together they constitute a specialized instrument for adaptation and readjustments in reactions as needs and situations change. Because of this receptivity to change, experience and use, apart from reasoning, can shape nervous connections and adjust reflexes. Simple sensory motor experience seems to count far more than reason in the actual process of acquiring new motor skills.

Behavior and Its Development

Behavior is an organismic reaction to changes in the environment. Initially, the ability to react to such changes (stimuli) is genetic. Connections exist between changes in the environment and response mechanisms of the organism. These connections are elaborated as the action is repeated (exercise). Initial responses—reflexes—to unconditioned stimuli are formed as inherited connections are reinforced and strengthened.

When we use passive and reflexive activity programs with our clients, we are actually utilizing these primary connections and establishing, or reestablishing, reflexes. As new stimuli (conditioned stimuli) become associated with the activity or response, temporary connections are made between these new external stimuli and the action or movement taking place. Eventually, after much repetition, these temporary connections become permanent. The individual is able now to respond with new behavior to a broader range of stimuli.

In addition, if we reward or punish each response contiguous to the activity, we will increase or decrease the possibility of that response occurring again under the same conditions. The inhibitory centers, in particular, are strengthened by aversive conditioning.

The whole mechanism of voluntary movement involves a concurrent linking of unconditioned and conditioned signals with rewards, lack of rewards, or punishment for the response performed. This linking strengthens those connections to responses that may be either active and goal attaining or passive and avoiding. It gradually results in connections that contain excitory and inhibitory memory components and components that render an object desirable or undesirable. Thus the object is given a positive (drawing) goal quality or an aversive (pushing away) goal quality. The entire process is one of association. Once the organism acquires new skills, he is able to respond and, under the same conditions, reproduce that activity.

CHAPTER IX

Effecting Communication
And Interaction

Most methods of habilitating the brain-injured, retarded, and profoundly handicapped have proved inadequate and insufficient. They treat the child on the basis of chronological age and I.Q. level. By accepting only the level the child presents, they fail to attempt ways of advancing his level of development and increasing his ability to achieve. Because an individual's ability to communicate and interrelate depends on his level of awareness, the profoundly handicapped must often stand outside their world. Only by augmenting and utilizing as fully as possible all his mechanisms of focus and attention can a child arrive at a point of readiness to communicate and relate.

We at the Institutes feel it is critically important to enable the child to reach and maintain this readiness to communicate. By developing all his potential and learning how to use it, a child can participate in and belong to the world around him.

Awareness, Focus, and Attention

Awareness

An individual is said to be "aware" when he can relate to his environment generally and not just to specific and direct stimuli. He is able to react to sounds, movement, and the presence of others in a meaningful way. Lacking this ability he may relate reflexively only to immediate and direct stimuli, such as cold, heat, and pain. He remains shut out of the human world.

Pavlov demonstrated that there is a lack of effect and relationship to the environment in the decorticated organism. In some profoundly retarded children with undertoned muscles (hypotonia) for example, there is often a lack of startle response, particularly when they are lying down. This is the kind of child one finds in the infirmaries of state institutions. The institutional policy of keeping these children in bed only makes the condition worse. The infrequent changes that might occur in their day-to-day environment may occasionally elicit some random activity—a sign of momentary awareness. But these children are unable almost completely to respond to specific noises or stimuli.

The picture these children present is quite similar to the early stages of human ontogenesis. We find such responses in the neonate and in the very young infant. However, we will find decreased states of awareness in any condition where the cortex is immature or has lost its ability to mediate and process input from lower neural and humoral systems.

The clinical and experimental literature in neurophysiology substantiates this relationship between cortical stimulation and awareness. Burns Adrian, Marruzzi, and Eccles have demonstrated the presence of a *central excitory system* located in the hypothalamus. Incoming stimuli of fairly low intensity to this region resulted in high levels of stimulation to the cerebral cortex. This led to arousal and awareness in the organism. This would also indicate that, where the central nervous system remains intact, the many subsystems are mediated. Stimuli from a central excitory system is integrated and balanced by a *central inhibitory system,* also located in the hypothalamus.

We have found that a program of exercise and training such as we employ at the Institutes does not have a profound effect on the neurologically intact individual's level of awareness. In those individuals who have sustained damage to the cortex, however, lower order reflexes will often be seen. Because they are directly related to higher level reflexes, we utilize these lower order reflexes (innate releasor mechanisms) to reach an increased state of integration, arousal, and awareness for the client.

> Peter, a three-year-old mongoloid child, was very hypotonic. He was unable to walk or stand; when placed on his stomach he could not raise his head.
>
> Peter did not respond in any noticeable fashion to the program of speech, physical and occupational therapy, tutoring, or recreational activities he was receiving. When we sat him up he would cry, but he did not respond to any specific stimuli we presented.
>
> We then placed Peter with his back to the wall for support, supported his chest, and brought his knees to hyperextension, putting full weight and pressure over his feet. His eyes widened, his crying ceased. He turned his head in the direction of a bell sound and towards wherever we called to him.
>
> Another problem was that we were unable to wake Peter up by ringing a bell. However, when we exercised his back extensor reflexes, he began to raise his head. After using this method for awhile, we noticed increased muscle tone in his back. Through stimulation and exercising these basic reflexes, Peter became aware. He could now raise his head and turn it toward the direction of any sound we presented.

These activities elicit the stretch reflex mechanisms at the ball of the foot, then facilitate them as each muscle stretches with the gravitational pull and the swift hyperextension of the knees. These mechanisms account for a tremendous volley of stimuli going into the central excitory system.

> We used the same principles to treat several patients in deep coma subsequent to chemopallidectomies for Parkinsonism. Neither prob-ing nor scratch-testing produced a state of awareness in them. We placed each patient on a tilt table and brought them to a full standing position passively, then quickly hyperextended the knees. At this exact moment, each patient became fully aware and could talk and communicate. But as soon as we lowered them back down to a sleep-ing position, the coma returned.
>
> We treated these patients daily, gradually weaning them from the comatose state. As they became conscious for longer and longer periods of time, their levels of awareness and interaction increased. Gradually, they were able to achieve this consciousness and awareness independently.

Seizures: The Gootzeit Maneuver for Treatment

> We use these stretch reflex contractions that are elicited upon standing in our work. They stimulate the cortex and strengthen and increase awareness and the ability to control lower reflexes. The techniques used to help Peter reach awareness and to bring the deep coma, chemopallidectomy patients to consciousness employ the same principles to treat a client in seizure. Many of our clients suffer from seizures. At the least, these can be disrupting to partici-pation in everyday activities, at worst; they can be life threatening.
>
> We treat *a small child* who has just gone into seizure by holding him upright and bracing him against a wall for support. We then hyperextend his knees against this wall and bring pressure over the balls of his feet by pressing down with the thumbs over his knees. If two people are available, one can provide support for the child while the other works on his knees. When this is done as soon as possible after the seizure begins, the child will most often return to consciousness quickly.
>
> When *an older client* begins to have a seizure it is usually necessary to treat him on the floor or table. His knees are hyperextended against the floor while the teacher presses rapidly in with the thumb on the ball of the foot, holding the foot at stretch. This is done with a light, pumping action.
>
> *Another procedure* that can be done with either a child or an adult who is going into seizure is for the teacher to press his hand against the angle of the upper and lower jaws, fingers on either side of the client's mouth. This clears a breathing passage for the client and most often interrupts the seizure and returns him to awareness.

Burns, Katz, Marruzzi, and Eccles conducted research on the stretch reflex mechanism and its effect on the central excitory system in the hypothalamus. Eccles produced alertness in surgically comatose cats by striking the ball of the foot. This area is an important center for eliciting stimuli to the CES. Thus, the technique we use at the Institutes for treating seizures elicits these stimuli and increases the incoming levels of stimuli to the CES. The stretch reflex mechanism employed by hyperextending the knees and pumping the foot at stretch, or putting weight and pressure over the ball of the foot, also results in high levels of stimulation to the cerebral cortex. This is usually sufficient to bring a client in seizure back to consciousness.

The period of postseizure activity for the client may range from being able to return to class or work immediately to the more typical experience of sleepiness. The seizure itself and its consequences, however, are drastically reduced. For the client, his family and those around him, his sense of well-being, physical safety, and ability to participae in everyday life is greatly enhanced.

The stretch reflex system can be utilized also to heighten the ability to communicate in persons demonstrating low levels of awareness. Standing a child might bring him to a level of awareness in which he is ready to respond to speech activities. First, we might babble to the patient; he learns to babble in response. Through repetition the response grows stronger. Cortical integration is stimulated and both awareness and beginning speech become more widespread and responsive. The child thus assumes an increasingly active role in his world.

Thus, the mechanisms demonstrated by Marruzi, Eccles, Katz, and Burns are those directly related to eliciting awareness itself.

Focus

If the main problem for the underactive seems to be to develop expanded periods of awareness prior to focusing on events, the problem for the hyperactive is to maintain the ability to focus long enough for perception and understanding to occur. The retarded and hyperactive child fails to pick up specific tones of visual cues. He may react massively to a single flashing light, groaning and screaming and running around the room. We need to narrow the range of sensory modalities to a specific object or situation. Only then will he focus on a particular event and learn.

Initially, it is necessary to eliminate distractions and background noise. We may also physically hold the child by the hand or on the lap or place him in a position from which he cannot escape—for example, sitting on a bench against the wall with the table pushed to the corner and up close to him. By limiting the amount of stimuli, and conditioning and reinforcing a narrow range of appropriate responses, we gradually eliminate much of the random behavior. The stimulus-response relationship becomes more and more specific and appropriate. The child is gradually able to focus more and more on the object or event. As people and things in his world come to have more meaning for him, he is able to understand and respond. Now, he can begin to interact.

While chemotherapy also reduces hyperactivity, we have found that we can fatigue out the random behavior with high energy games and swimming. Children who have participated in this activity in the morning are able to sit longer and more quietly for arts and crafts or classsroom activity in the afternoon. We were also more successful with speech therapy at this time. Focus time was increased and random activity diminished noticeably using this technique.

As an individual's focus time and attention span increase, we attempt to habituate him to a less isolated, more realistic environment. We slowly accustom him to a noisier background more like that of his home and neighborhood. As we continue to elicit and reinforce attention to foreground stimuli, the background stimuli loses its power to distract. The child works more in groups, surrounded by other activities. He gradually becomes less hyperactive. Noise and activity that were once distracting and disabling now become meaningless.

Once the child, whether underactive or overactive, becomes functional in more normal environments, he assumes a more meaningful role in his day-to-day world, both in school and at home. He is more able to react and communicate and, thus, to interact with people and situations. As a consequence, he elicits even further and more positive responses from those around him. His range of experiences and learning is broadened and the process itself becomes self-generating and self-rewarding.

Attention and Habituation

Using awareness and the ability to focus, an individual must hold his attention to a situation or event long enough to understand it and to respond to it. As he attempts to do this, all the sensory modalities become tuned to the specific object or event. This, in turn, augments and evokes more and more of his stored information. Memory systems are activated and reinforced. The individual now derives meaning from situations. He begins to perceive and to learn.

We use this effort especially to modify speech ability. We vary the length and type of speech signals to increase the range of perception. Thus the individual becomes more able to communicate on a larger scale.

We have also found it important to have the head turned in the direction of the stimulus. We may begin the process by actually turning the child's head for him. This seems to tune his hearing and visual modalities to the event. As he accumulates and stores more information, the proprioceptive and motor abilities are also elicited and become directed towards the stimulus. He learns to react in a more coordinated and effective manner.

CHAPTER X

Behavior Modification
(With Rose Marie Hughes)

Systems of Behavior Modification

Essentially, any system used to intentionally change behavior can be termed "behavior modification." Among the effective systems of behavior modification are:

1. Modification via acculturation, education, and guidance.

2. Behavioral systems:
   a. The laws of Exercise, Readiness, and Spread of Effect.
   b. Classical conditioning
   c. Operant conditioning (including reward, punishment, and extinction).

3. Psychodynamic systems:
   a. Freudian
   b. Horney
   c. Jungian
   d. Adlerian
   e. Rogerian
   f. Others

4. Chemical and drug techniques

5. Surgical systems

Most behavior evolves via acculturative means. That is, we create an environment for learning—classroom, swimming pool, playground, workshop, play group—and devote time and attention to wanted behavior. Behavioral changes take place via play, repetition of action (rehearsal or exercise), and the affect (pleasure or displeasure) that follows each activity. Yet these changes cannot be attributable to any specific activity. The specific moment-to-moment behaviors and their causes are not usually attended to or recorded in these everyday life situations. These situations are concurrent or sequential and do not affect behavior specifically. Rather, the general broad activity, its subject matter, and the results effected are considered most important.

Play and fantasy, for instance, are rehearsals for real life activities; a form of exercise that strengthens behavior connections. The characteristics of the cultural process guide the directions of the play activities, thereby patterning elementary behaviors as well as complex outlooks.

The educational process offers a graded presentation of materials and experiences on an individual and group basis. Further modification of behavior is effected as each individual acquires new action possibilities. When specific individual problems arise in the attempt to learn ways of behavior acceptable to society, guidance and educative techniques are often used to better help that person meet the demands of his society.

Major behavioral changes in people occur, therefore, through acculturation, rehearsal and play, education and guidance. On a day-to-day basis, teachers and other professionals utilize all the systems of behavior modification, including classical and operant conditioning and psychodynamics. This is a nonselective basis for action and intervention because it represents a "common-sense" approach to changing behavior. Such an approach effects the environment and structure of the individual and, as such, is one more method that can broadly be called "acculturative."

There are special situations that occur, however, and require a more specific approach. Problems in learning and emotional disturbances require a more structured method, one that goes into the theoretical and practical systems of behavior modification to focus and ameliorate the particular problem presented. This is true whether the individual is a child or adult, handicapped or not.

In line with this approach, our methods at the Institutes for Applied Human Dynamics involve a neo-Hullian system of behavior modification: by integrating other systems, we attempt to account for all the dynamic planes of behavior. Given a behavior apparatus, one which is genetically inherited and elaborated during the lifetime of each individual, we can begin to describe the organization of our system.

The Gootzeit System: An Adaptation from a Neo-Hullian Concept of Behavior

Unlearned Reflex Connections

We all begin with an unlearned potential to react to changes in the environment: sU_R (unlearned behavior potential). During the main fetal stage, the only environmental changes that occur are those of temperature, electrodynamics, chemical changes in the mother's blood, and mechanical (vibrational or pressure) changes that impinge directly on the body surface of the fetus.

The initial responses, R, are stereotyped and massive in nature. As the fetal nervous system matures, the responses and inherited sensory connections become more specific. As a result, we have the emergence of unconditioned reflexes. These reflexes are phylogenetic in nature—the actions are related to survival, both in the fetal fluid environment and in accordance with earlier sequences of evolutionary development. This latter process is related to a sequence of segmental nonvertebral, vertebral, amphibian, reptilian, mammalian, and, finally, human origins.

At birth almost all the reaction potentials (sUR) are unlearned: inherited, unlearned connections between changes in the environment (sUR—unconditional stimuli) and inherited, unlearned responses (UR—not related to experience). We can summarize these by the following:

$$*sU_R = \text{Unlearned Elicitation}$$
$$*sU_R = \text{Unlearned Connections}$$
$$*sE_R = \text{Learned Connections}$$

These first two have had their origin in the hereditary mechanisms and in changes in the immediate internal and external environments of the mother's womb. The last event occurs only in relation to experience, using all of the former mechanisms in the learning process. Connections are strengthened by action as changes elicit responses and effect the related physical structures and functions.

Immediately after birth the neonate enters an unconditioned, reflexive state of affairs. The physiological systems that were adequate for intrauterine life now become inadequate. Even as the placenta begins to disconnect, the carbon dioxide content of the baby's blood increases. This, in turn, increases heart action and blood pressure. It becomes urgent for the respiratory system to start activity: whether reflexly, by internal humoral mechanism or, immediately after birth by jarring, as the baby falls or is smacked lightly by the physician. The lungs now begin to function for the first time via the appropriate innate releasor mechanisms (IRM's).

From this moment on, the placenta can no longer furnish the oxygen and nutritional and expulsive needs of the infant. Innate chemical stimulus mechanisms are now set into operation and modified by the need for oxygen and the first few drops of water placed on the baby's lips. The functions of the lungs, kidneys, and urogenital systems are released as the first demands for oxygen exchange and elimination of water and waste press on the distended bladder. The nutrients taken into the system also stimulate the need for elimination. Thus a dramatic change in the living state—from fetus to infant—immediately elicits a whole group of inherited reflexes.

As conditions elicit these innate releasor mechanisms (IRM's), certain basic fixed action patterns (FAP) are also stimulated; the first breathing and sucking actions, for example. Repetition of these basic responses to the changes of states within the organism strengthens inherited connections. These are illustrations of Thorndike's old Law of Exercise, which we feel is still pertinent.

Needs and Neural Behavior Nets

The fetus has its needs for warmth, nutrition, and elimination met by the maternal environment. While it is known that a probe can elicit evasive movement from the fetus, in the natural state it is rare that such action is necessary. Usually this occurs when the mother has been inactive, in one position for a long period of time, and the fetus becomes cramped or uncomfortable.

Immediately after birth, however, a number of concurrent behavior needs are set in motion through the action of neural behavior nets (NBN). Coelentrates (jellyfish), for example, possess neural behavior nets that permit:

1. Complete action for fight and flight;
2. Complete action for food getting and elimination.

In contrast, the human baby has a much larger number of neural behavior nets that are instantly set into motion:

1. Actions to get food;
2. Actions to get attention;
3. Actions to be cleaned;
4. Actions to be held.

Later, these basic nets will involve neural behavior nets for play, playmates, movement, dominance, territorial imperatives, and so forth.

Each of the behavior nets initially in effect at birth are alerted, prepared, and readied for action by *a state of need*. We can express these basic need states thus:

1. The seconds of privation (hp). For example, oxygen = $*hOx$ = hours of privation of oxygen.
2. The time elapsed of water privation (hw = hours of water privation).
3. The hours of privation of food (hf = hours of food privation).
4. The hours of privation of mother (hm = hours of mother's absence).

Drive States

The needs discussed above set up internal states of excitement or stimulation that we call *drives* (D) or *drive states* (sD). Beyond basic needs such as breathing, heart rate, etc., the organism can respond to only one need at a time. A competition arises, therefore, among drives (D), drive states (sD), and *drive conditions* (CD). The strongest drive (sD'), in terms of its primary value, releases a neural behavior net (NBN) for action. This engages the organism in a search for stimuli or images (SFI) that are relevant to the most dominant need of the moment.

If we wish to set up drive states (sD), we first determine what states of privation we can manipulate. We then set up levels of privation (hp) to obtain an increase in the intensity or frequency of the need for the organism to respond to what it is being deprived of, and use the appropriate neural behavior net to do so.

Once a drive state is elicited and stimuli relevant to the neural nets are presented, we can elicit responses of various types, including initial inherited responses. These can include:

1. Fixed motor patterns (FMP), which cause arm and leg movement.

2. Responses resulting from emotional expression (EmEx).

3. Autonomic responses such as galvanic skin responses (GSR) and heart rate (HR).

4. Salivation (Sal).

5. Vocalization (Voc).

6. Urination (Ur).

7. Sweating (Sw).

8. Facial expressions (FaEx).

9. Tonic motor acts (TMA).

10. Aggressive behavior (AgB).

11. Affectionate behavior (AfB).

The active responses can be observed or considered to be taking place on a horizontal or vertical plane, in place, during eating, as a waking or arousal response, as a scanning or searching response.

Conditioned Stimulus

When a drive state (sD), a stimulus related directly to a neural behavior net (NBN)—words, signs, gestures—or a conditioned stimulus is presented concurrently with the primary, unconditioned stimulus (UCS), we have a linking of that conditional stimulus (CS) to the response (R). This stage is called the *Classical Conditioning state of affairs*. From this relationship arise the ontogenetic beginnings of behavior. A linkage to experience and changes in the distal environment occurs, to which the organism now responds.

The following illustrates the conditioning process we have been discussing:

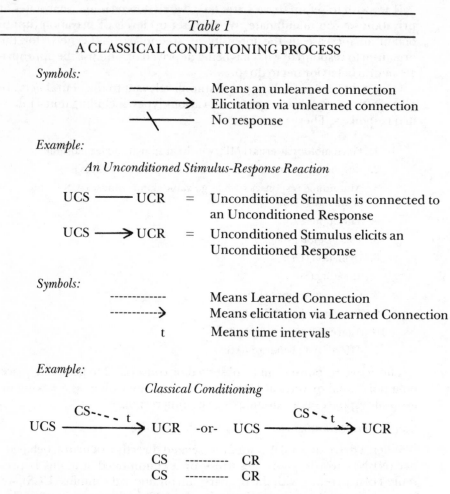

Table 1

A CLASSICAL CONDITIONING PROCESS

Symbols:

——————   Means an unlearned connection
————→   Elicitation via unlearned connection
——┤———   No response

Example:

An Unconditioned Stimulus-Response Reaction

UCS ——— UCR   =   Unconditioned Stimulus is connected to
an Unconditioned Response

UCS ——→ UCR   =   Unconditioned Stimulus elicits an
Unconditioned Response

Symbols:

- - - - - - -   Means Learned Connection
- - - - - →   Means elicitation via Learned Connection
t   Means time intervals

Example:

Classical Conditioning

$$\text{UCS} \xrightarrow{\quad CS\text{- - -}_t\quad} \text{UCR} \quad \text{-or-} \quad \text{UCS} \xrightarrow{\quad CS\text{- -}_t\quad} \text{UCR}$$

CS - - - - - CR
CS - - - - - CR

It is from these relationships of classical conditioning that we must seek how words, symbols, and gestures can be substituted for primary drive stimuli and needs so that we can elicit behaviors by conditioned stimuli. When we speak of classical conditioning, therefore, we are speaking of stimulus substitution: the *word* "grape" elicits a *food* response; rather than actually putting a grape in the mouth, which elicits an internal state of hunger and a salivation response.

Reinforcement and Operant Conditioning

Each initial response to a stimuli is quickly followed by a satisfying, unsatisfying, or painful state of affairs. Every response, thereafter—subsequent to an initial response—has rewarding, unrewarding, or punishing qualities. These qualities (feelings) can be further strengthened and enhanced if, together with the response, we give a reward (positive reinforcement); a nonreward (negative reinforcement); or a punishment (aversive conditioning). From this point we develop a conditioned reaction potential (*sER).

The effect of reinforcement (N) or punishment (K-) given contiguously to a response strengthens the possibility of that response occurring again, if desired; or ceasing to occur, if unwanted (extinction); or diminishing significantly, if aversively conditioned. This method of behavior modificaton is called *Operant (or Instrumental) Conditioning* and illustrates Thorndike's new Law of Exercise: responses that are reinforced (rewarded) and repeated are strengthened. We also feel that responses that are aversively conditioned are diminished or extinguished.

Habituation

When a stimulus is given at a constant interval over a period of time, an inhibition sets in. Conditioned or unconditioned stimuli will not be conducted. They will fail, therefore, to elicit a response. Similarly, if a response is not rewarded or is punished, under given constant conditions, it will become meaningless. That is, under the same circumstances, the desired response will not occur. This constant environmental condition (CEC) and constant state of affairs results in an inhibitory state known as *habituation*. Once this occurs, futher stimuli are neither received nor will they elicit a response.

When used initially, a stimuli (S), goal object (G), incentives, (K) and reinforcements (N+), have short term novelty properties (stn). Used over and over again, they develop long term novelty qualities (ltn), including the ability to elicit habituation. For example, if a child has never tasted "M & M" candies, he might not respond to them. Once he tastes them, however, the candy develops a short term novelty quality—stn—and can be used as a goal object (G), eliciting certain behaviors directed to attaining the object as a reinforcement (N+). As such it can be used as a reward after performing some desired task. It may also be used as a goal object itself, in which the child must perform in order to obtain the candy. Thus, it takes on stimulus as well as reinforcement properties.

If we give too many M&M's, the child becomes sated, privation (hp) drops; drive (D) lessens. Either he may not respond (R-) or the M&M's may take on an aversive, punishing quality (K-). After several days of this, the M&M's acquire long term novelty properties and the child ceases to respond to them in the same way, at the same speed. In fact, he may reject the candy as soon as it is presented. This is a sign of habituation (CEC). A similar example occurs when a hungry infant eagerly sucks at his mother's breast. Once filled, however, he may bite or pull back his head; the breast has become aversive to him.

In everyday life, habituation functions to block out meaningless stimuli: situations that do not meet a need or drive state. Thus, at the Institutes we expose a child to an intense stimulus environment. Eventually, meaningless stimuli are blocked and the child can concentrate on new stimuli and new situations. The dulling or elimination of background noise is just as important to the child's functioning as the need to discover how to intensify the stimulus properties (SP) of pertinent stimuli. However, even meaningful stimuli can be blocked out or habituationed if reception of the stimuli does not result in satisfaction and consequential drive reduction.

The tactics used at the Institutes have resulted in hundreds of children learning to walk, talk, or decrease their hyperactivity. It has also enabled individuals with catastrophic acting out behavior finally learning to function and maintain themselves in a community program, outside institutional walls.

Some Examples of the Gootzeit Techniques

The Institutes uses the neural behavior net techniques in a number of radical situations:

> Bill was a ten-year-old, nonverbal, autistic child. We took him into the swimming pool to chin-deep level and disengaged the therapist's hands from his grip. Immediately, this random, autistic child made eye contact. He began to bounce off the bottom of the pool, where the water was now slightly over his head, by light jumps and hops. Having thus survived, in less than an hour he was bouncing and jumping up and down of his own accord. He still was unable to get out of the pool however. Now frustrated and tensed, he broke into his first known, clear speech: "Get me the hell out of here!"
>
> Three weeks later, Bill was an independent swimmer. More importantly, he was talking.

We have tried this technique with many children over the years. Almost all have learned to swim and many, in their need to survive, have spoken. The frequency of eye contact was also increased tremendously.

Gootzeit Behavioral Modification Techniques

At the Institutes of Applied Human Dynamics we do not separate our behavior modification system into theoretical and practical units, as is often done in laboratory or experimental situations. In a classical laboratory system all variables can be stringently controlled. In such a case it may be of value to separate classical from operant conditioning or psychodynamic techniques. At the Institutes, however, we combine and use all behavior modification systems concurrently. We employ the following procedures, depending upon the level of function of a client. This level will determine what tactics will be used.

1. *If the client is aware and can function at some levels of independence,* we try psychodynamic and educational procedures. We attempt to find which neural behavior nets and drive states can be utilized to set the client into voluntary activity in the pursuit of educational tasks.

   Would the presence of a young woman motivate activity? Would a pat on the face elicit eye contact? If so, we can reinforce (N+) the action by food, reward, approbation, affection, or other supportive techniques.

2. *If the client is aggressive and acting out,* we would have to elicit his fear behavior net to effect withdrawal and evasive behavior (K-). Then, we would positively reinforce the withdrawal (N+) by the absence of approval. In an extreme situation, we might withdraw a food reinforcement or apply disapprobation as a form of punishment.

3. *If the client needs assistance to perform,* we try to determine in what areas he is already successfully independent. We then increase and enlarge those areas of independent action with operant, positive reinforcement or we aversively condition unwanted behaviors. If the client can initiate, but not complete, an action, we reinforce each initial aspect (N+). As he acquires additional aspects of the action, we continue to reinforce each new step. This is known as *shaping.* By this process, each response is strengthened and achieved more quickly, until the complete, desired response is performed voluntarily.

4. *If the client is less independent,* we passive-assistively aid him to act: we might take his hand and join with him in a circle dance; we might start the spoon to his lips and let him complete the action. We then reward it. If he cannot complete the action, we switch to neurodevelopmental tactics. Using passive or reflexive activity and shaping, we operantly reinforce his efforts, hoping that this will lead gradually to more skilled and independent actions.

5. *If we cannot obtain a voluntary action from the dependent type of child,* we switch totally to neurodevelopmental tactics. We can then elicit the reaction reflexly. When the response finally occurs, we operantly reinforce it. Classically, in neurodevelopmental terms, we first evoke the action and then give the response a reward — an example of operant conditioning.

These techniques augment those which utilize neurodevelopmental methods. Together they increase ten-thousand-fold the frequency of initial and correct responses. The rewards strengthen the possibility of the action occurring in other situations. In contrast, traditional operant conditioning first waits until the response (R+) appears before attempting to reinforce it. Classical conditioning does not operantly reinforce the response, as this is not pertinent to the conditioning process. Instead, conditioning occurs by stimulus substitution.

The primary technique for developing eye contact, used at the Institutes, is to place the hand on the child's cheek and gaze into his eyes. Reinforcement is given by patting his head or smiling. Other techniques include holding the child in the breast feeding position; the child will peer reflexly into the holder's eyes.

If reflexive activation fails, we employ passive activity methods, since *every* movement results in the physiological improvement of the condition.

In addition, there are those behaviors that we want to decrease or eliminate. Should we want to elicit a decrement of response, we first negatively reinforce (N-) the response. We do not reward it at all. If the behavior persists, we aversively conditon (K-) or punish it. For example, if Johnny keeps throwing blocks on the floor, we may first isolate him (time out). If this is not effective, or if the block throwing increases, we then restrict manually or aversively condition Johnny's movements. This results in a decrement of the unwanted behavior.

We call our technique a *bracket—a bracket for performance*. That is, we elicit an action by classical means and close the bracket by reinforcing or aversively conditioning every response elicited by the stimulus. Using this technique, we increase dramatically our chances of reinforcing an event because we can elicit it on demand. Later we introduce interval reinforcement and, finally, periodic reinforcement. By so doing, we can eventually release the response from dependency upon a reward or punishment.

Acting Up Individuals

A number of clients at the Institutes have histories of acting up behavior. These clients are considered severely and profoundly handicapped because they are untestable and because of their violent, tantrum behavior.

> —Jimmy is a schizophrenic eighteen-year-old. He attends our school, evening, and Saturday programs. He periodically hits his mother and seventy-year-old father and pulls their house apart. He was first institutionalized at Bronx Children's Pschiatric Hospital and later at Bronx State Psychiatric Hospital.

—John is a twenty-year-old who periodically tears his house apart and has, on occasion, caused multiple facial injuries and bruises to his mother.

—Billy, twenty-one years old, regularly takes his food tray and throws it on others in the cafeteria line.

—Jenny has torn off her clothes at programs and in the street.

Behavior modification for these and other acting up individuals starts with a directive, acculturative technique. This demands regular attendance at programs from the client. Despite incidences of tantrums or acting up, he can never be sent out of program or barred from returning.

The day-to-day program routines provide an opportunity to participate in a range of activities throughout the day (also in evening and weekend programs). This affords the client a means to join others in group activity, to interact, and to measure up to group requirements for activity and living. This is the most frequently used method of modifying behavior, and the most effective in meeting the day-to-day life needs of the client.

There are times, however, when these clients will act up. They may break furniture, windows, or hit other clients, endangering their well-being. Or they may hit out or attack staff members. When this occurs we take special care to analyze the basis of these events, if possible. We also take into account the client's assets and how to deflect the acting up and prevent injury or damage to persons and property.

First, if any clients begin to show signs of agitation, we place them under a one-to-one observation. We do not exclude them from the group, however. If they continue to participate constructively in the program, we give them approbation, recognition, pay, and/or instant sweet reinforcers, as the case indicates.

Usually, we insist on the clients continuing the program. We do not permit withdrawal as, in our experience, unwanted behaviors seem to be positively reinforced and increase in frequency by withdrawal. When handled in this manner, the behavior may not be completely eliminated but it declines in frequency.

When acting up does occur and we cannot prevent it, we use the following sequence of aversive steps:

1. Disapprobation
2. Taking the role of Ogre, hovering and threatening and bossy. Often the client is threatened in strong commanding tones until the unwanted behavior ceases. Of course, the staff is trained to present such as appearance.
3. If a violent event occurs, we use a sequence of Gootzeit techniques, described below, to control the client.

4. If all else fails, we use prescriptive aversive electrical techniques. This is rarely used and only by prescription by a team composed of a physician, psychologist, social worker and the Executive Director—and always with parental consent. Should this technique be employed, care must be taken to give only one or two shocks. After this, the mere presence of the device or its buzzer provokes fear and is the most effective at this level.

Not all clients are affected by the device, of course, and frequently, persons shocked adjust to pain and will be unaffected by further treatment. Nevertheless, the use of blows or hitting is dangerous as an aversive measure, since the intensity of force used cannot be measured or governed at each instance. The intensity of the electrical device, however, is controlled and limited by the design of the instrument itself.

Specific Gootzeit Techniques for Controlling an Acting Up Individual

The techniques we describe are actually adaptations from lifesaving procedures. Essentially, they are used to control the acting up individual until he is able to calm himself and return to the program activity. These techniques, when properly rendered, afford a maximum of control while not damaging the client.

Procedure One (Cross-Chest)

Whenever possible, always approach an acting up client from the rear. If he is small enough in size, place him in the cross-chest position with your arm over his shoulder and your hip into his back. Use the other arm to prevent him from scratching. (See Fig. 17)

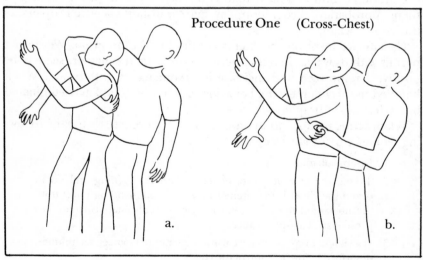

Fig. 17

Procedure Two
If the client is standing, bring him down from behind using one hand on his head for leverage and the other hand to support his back, to prevent too swift a descent and possible injury. If he is too resistive, use two hands on his forehead to bring him down. *(See Fig. 18)*

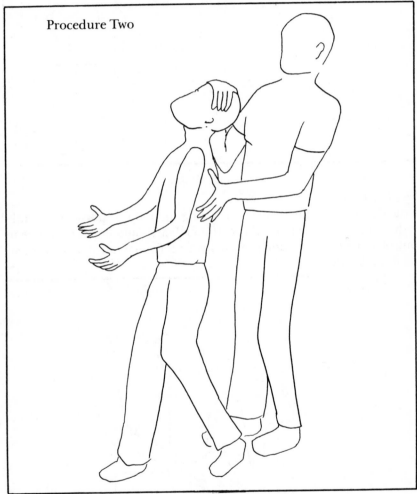

Procedure Two

Fig. 18

Procedure Three
If the client is now on the ground but continues to act up, one or more workers must pin his arms or shoulders—and legs, if necessary—to the floor, holding him there until he can calm down. *(See Fig. 19)*

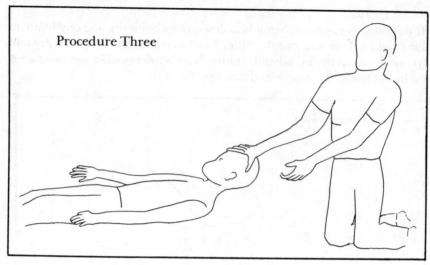

Fig. 19

Procedure Four

If the client is standing while he is acting up and it is possible to gently push him back over a table, the staff member should do so. Continue to control him on the table and prevent his arms from scratching the worker. *(See Fig. 20a-20b)*

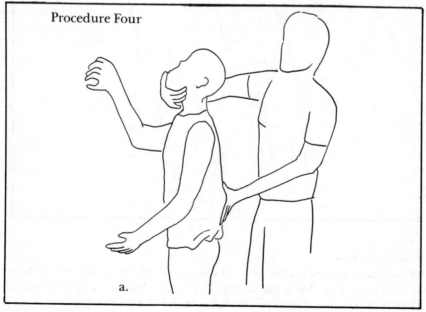

Fig. 20 (a)

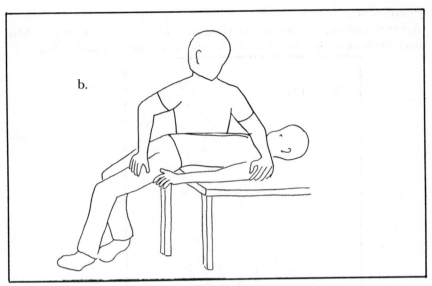

Fig. 20 (b)

Procedure Five

Another controlling technique is to back the client into an armchair. With a hand on his chin, using the lifesaving childhold, tilt his head back. If possible, place padding on the back of the chair to soften the effects of the pressure. *(See Fig. 21)*

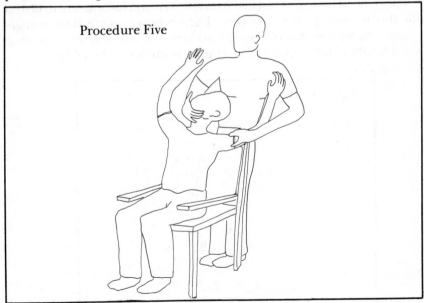

Procedure Five

Fig. 21

Procedure Six
Another technique utilizing the chair is to hold both arms of the client over the back of the chair until he is able to calm down. *(See Fig. 22)*

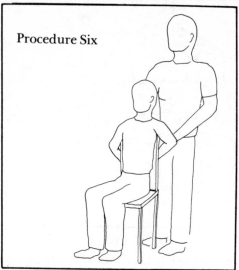

Procedure Six

Fig. 22

Procedure Seven (Long Control Method)
Another technique to calm a child is one in which the worker or parent sits comfortably on a chair. The child is on the floor and his arms are held over the thighs and legs of the worker. The worker's legs are then brought around the body of the child, over his thighs. With the worker's feet set on the floor, the child's legs are locked underneath the worker's legs. *(See Fig. 23)*

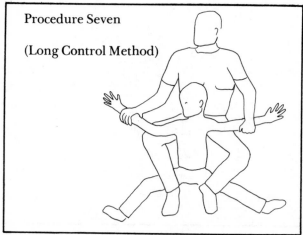

Procedure Seven

(Long Control Method)

Fig. 23

Procedure Eight (Block and Parry)
Should a client make an extremely hostile approach to the front of a worker, the "block and parry" technique can be used for protection.

As the client advances, the worker quickly extends his arm, locks his elbow into place, and puts one hand just above the sternum of the client. Then, he pushes the client backwards (blocking). If the worker can act quickly enough, he cups the client's arm above the elbow with his other arm and swings the client around to face in the opposite direction (parry). *(See Fig. 24)*

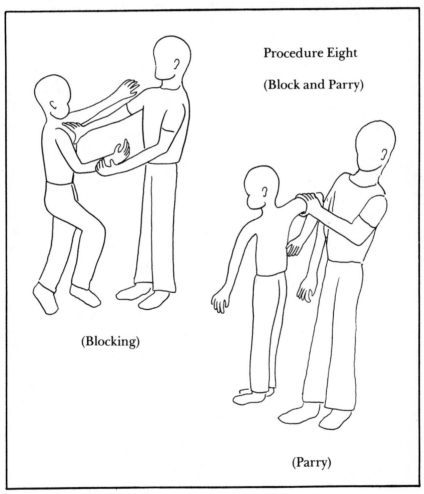

Procedure Eight

(Block and Parry)

(Blocking)

(Parry)

Fig. 24

Pavlov spoke of a "freedom reflex." He found that his dogs preferred to stand rigidly and take his experimental procedures without moving, rather than be held down by straps. When we hold down an acting up client it is an aversive technique, one that helps to stop acting up behavior when it occurs. The threat of restraint has often been sufficient to prevent many instances of tantrum behavior.

In concluding this section, we must reiterate that we have never dropped a client from a program because of the severity of his disability, even such extreme behaviors as we have just described. The twenty years of experience that has helped so many of our clients to progress only demonstrates the effectiveness of our principles and techniques.

CHAPTER XI

Effecting Purposive Activity

The main task of rehabilitation workers with the functionally retarded and brain-injured child, and the prerequisite for their further development, is to motivate the child to deal with his environment in an adaptive and adjustive manner. The methods described in this chapter to elicit responses and adjustments to environment are used extensively with many retarded at the Institutes of Applied Human Dynamics and its centers for the handicapped. The methods we have found most effective emphasize and develop activity-provoking situations of a nonverbal or anxiety-provoking nature, which force the child to deal with his environment in an effective problem-solving manner. These methods have been found to be effective with all our children but are most successful with those retarded who are severely impaired emotionally, yet whose potential for intellectual growth is good.

Determination of good intellectual growth potential is made in one of two ways. First, a potential for intellectual growth is assumed when there is an available medical diagnosis of emotional disturbance, schizophrenia, autism, etc., as the primary cause of functional retardation. Second, the potential is assumed if, as a result of an initial use of the technique, a swifter reaction and adaption to the environment is found in a child, more so than in other children who react but adapt at a slower pace. The second determination, therefore, is based on ability to learn and function rather than on I.Q. or a diagnostic category.

The activities at the Institute are, in large part, the same as those used extensively in any good educational and recreational program. They include object relations, games, rhythms and dance, use of letters and blocks, etc. The primary component differentiating the Institute's program from other programs is that we at the Institute are directive. That is, the child MUST participate in an assigned activity. If the child participates, he can do so at his own pace and interest. If he does not, however, he will be made to participate by some passive-assistance or forced means.

The directive method achieves a behavioral reaction because the situation or stimulus provided must be reached in order to achieve safety, comfort, or survival. If there is no reaction, the child is passive-assistively made to follow through the activity until an active participation (degree by degree) is elicited. In other words, the child must react with or without volition.

Learning takes place through: (1) the utilization of classical conditioning techniques (stimulus substitution); (2) the application of positive reinforcement or aversive conditioning, resulting in the eliciting of wanted behavior with increased frequency or decreasing the frequency of unwanted behavior; and (3) the forced action of elicitor mechanisms and/or evoking of certain behaviors via training through passive-assistive techniques and constant repetitive activity.

Working with severely involved, brain-injured, and functionally retarded individuals offers us a unique opportunity to deal with the genesis of purposive behavior and the initial phases of learning. In this chapter, we deal with children who typically wander randomly or who have difficulty in developing purposive action because of their hyperactivity.

Many of these children can be found in institution infirmaries or in day centers for the severely retarded in the community. Workers in the field usually have difficulty in involving them in any purposive activity as they wander or dash about aimlessly. We often involve them by passive-assistive methods but have great difficulty in eliciting a directed action.

Effecting Object Relations

It is interesting to observe that in most instances, these children can identify food objects of all types from nonfood objects. For example, if we give Ruth a series of blocks and shapes, she plays with them randomly, comveying some to her mouth. If we then place a few grapes in with the blocks and shapes, Ruth will pick out all of the grapes first and convey only grapes to her mouth, ignoring the other objects. If we mix in apple slices, dried apricots, etc., she picks out all the food objects, discriminating them from the nonfood objects.

Another example is Debbie, who wanders aimlessly. On several occasions she was able to focus on a sandwich from across the room. Her blank expression changed in these instances to one of intense interest. This interest was quickly followed by swift, directed action in which she strode across the room, picked up the sandwich, and bit into it.

These children often demonstrate an ability to develop skills via operant learning, particularly when trying to evade confinement of a threatening situation.

Gene was stood in a corner with two tables placed so as to block his passage. These tables were held rigidly in position. A chair that was easily moved was placed at one end. Gene first wandered aimlessly then tried to push the tables away. When he came to the chair he was able to push it out and escape. Placing him back in the same position resulted in his escaping sooner. Escape was positively reinforced.

The presence of insight in relation to certain objects can be demonstrated in these children. Elena, who on most occasions seems to be a random wanderer, was taken into the swimming pool. She was permitted to sink and flail in the water for five seconds. She quickly made for the wall, climbed out of the pool, walked to a stone bench, picked up a towel and started to wipe herself. This was repeated several times with the same results.

We have been able to use classic conditioning to develop some initial object relations in a number of children of this kind. We were unable to get a number of these children to sit on chairs for a period of time as a prelude to including them in group or class activities. We used a low volt Faradic muscle stimulator and later, a shock prod, as an aversive stimulator for each child. If they tried to escape sitting for a required period, the stimulator would be held in place until the child sat. If the child attempted to rise, the stimulator was then reapplied. We then began to say, "sit!" quite sharply, just after the aversive shock and just before the sitting behavior. Eight children so conditioned can now enter a room and find a chair to sit on without instruction. Occasionally, when the behavior becomes random, a quick "sit!" command results in the desired action of picking out a chair for sitting. Thereafter, the shock need not be rendered. Merely the buzzing sound or the sight of the prod causes a fear reaction and an accommodation to the demand.

Eliciting of Color Relations

It is quite difficult to determine whether or not these children have color discrimination to begin with. We had Ruth's mother deny her food for twelve hours in order to elicit a hunger drive for our study. We then took two round lids as color objects, one red and one yellow, and placed a grape under the yellow lid. When Ruth reached toward the table, we placed a grape in her mouth. When she touched the yellow lid, we put a grape in her mouth and after 700 trials, when Rugh lifted the yellow lid she got her grape reward. Later the positions were changed and a blue lid was introduced, but Ruth was able to find the yellow lid and grape more frequently as the experiment was repeated. However, we could not elicit this activity in relation to nonfood objects.

Richard, a hyperactive youngster, was given a complicated task. Here a muffin tin was used. Red, black, yellow, and green discs were used to cover all the muffin wells in random order. We placed a grape under green discs only. After some trial and error, Richard would lift only green discs to get his grape. However, after eating a number of grapes (apparently sated) he again became random. We then gave him a cookie and placed cookies only under black discs. He quickly got the idea, and lifted only black discs until he once more became random when he apparently became sated.

The eliciting of these purposive activities seems to be epigenetic in character. The frequency of such tasks seems to be related to a growing ability in each of these children to solve new problems more swiftly and, in our judgment, they appear to be frequently more aware and purposive, even when removed from the study situations. Perhaps tasks of ascending demand are related to the development and emergence of intelligence in these severely impaired individuals.

Rationale for a Directive Method

The question that should now be asked is, what is the rationale of the directive method and why is it successful? The answer simply is that the impairment frequently found in retardation, brain injury, and emotional disturbance is the quantity and quality of reactiveness itself. Reactiveness is the very threshhold of behavior.

There are many reasons for this apparent reduction of reactiveness in these conditions. There may be (1) reduced levels of internal stimulation due to impairment of the reticular activating system or any of the tone-producing centers; (2) impairment stemming from attempts to manipulate objects in the environment that have met with failure and pain; or, (3) a certain embeddedness, as Schachtel terms it, due to some diminution of explorative behavior.

When analyzing the problems of these children through the lines of functioning behavior, the most glaring fault is evident. There is a reduction in activity and/or purposive activity. This information led us to the conclusion that some means must be found to elicit activity and eventually purposive activity. If this threshhold behavior could be elicited, behavior could be induced. For this reason, our directive methods of passive-assistive and forced activity were evolved to elicit this threshhold. When the activity occurred, either passively or later at any level, we rewarded that activity.

Because there is a great disparity between the verbal (when it exists) expression of the children and their apparent ability and willingness to become active once activity is induced by the directive techniques described, we have made the core of our methods an attempt to develop activity-evoking and anxiety-provoking situations of a nonverbal nature. The working and effect of our methods can best be illustrated by several case histories.

Michael, an autistic schizophrenic boy of eleven years, would sit or wander aimlessly with no apparent purposive relation to his environment. Almost six months were spent trying to get him to respond to voice instruction or to join games of his own volition. When Michael was brought to the swimming pool we noticed some attempts at avoidance behavior. When placed standing in shallow water, he would quickly go to the ladder and climb out. These were the first signs that Michael was able to react purposively and appropriately in his environment. With specially trained "therapist-water safety instructors" Michael was placed in deep water over his head. He had to jump up from the bottom in order to get his breath. As the bobbing continued, Michael began to flail to keep above water for more and more extended periods of time. At one point, while keeping his head above water, Michael said loudly and clearly, "Get me out of here!"

Michael was not taken out of the water, however, but made to solve the problem of learning to bob to the side of the pool in order to get out. Thus, activity was induced by the need to survive and the successful clearing of the head from the water was reinforced by Michael's ability to breathe. The fact that he had to deal with the environment resulted in a significant problem-solving event. Two weeks later, Michael was a proficient deep water swimmer. He talked during other activities (arts and crafts, rhythms and dance, etc.) quite frequently and by the end of the season was able to move on to a more nondirective and verbal-cored program.

Ben, a ten-year-old patient at Rockland State Hospital, was brought to our Institute's Saturday program by his parents. Ben would not join in group activity, would throw tantrums, or would run when we attempted to verbally direct him into activity. We passive-assistively forced him into activity. For example, Ben would be grabbed by either arm by a volunteer or assistant and practically dragged into round dances. During the first period, other volunteers would move each of his legs in a dance step and would relax in assisting him only when his legs would spontaneously move in conjunction and harmony with the other members of the group. After several sessions, Ben would join the group when a leader merely extended a hand and would then dance along with the others in apparent comfort and ease. Directiveness and passive-assistive techniques started in arts and crafts, swimming, etc., resulted in this child actively participating in a number of activity areas. During the activities, Ben is apparently at ease and happy and the level of autonomous activity has picked up significantly.

Susan is fourteen. She has been diagnosed as a schizophrenic retardate. She throws tantrums and frequently uses profanity to insult her mother and others she meets. Our initial contact with this youngster presented an individual who would not join in group activity. Any invitation to join in a game or activity was met with a "No!" and a tirade of vindictiveness and profanity.

At this point we started our directive process. We would force Susan into games and dances and passive-assistively move her through the motions until she would exhaust her resistance and join in. At times we were forced to insult her when she would sit down in the middle of a ramp and refuse to get up. We would ask her several times to get up and go into the program. When she refused, we merely grabbed one of her legs and literally dragged her in the direction of the activity room. Each yard or so we would ask her if she would get up and go herself. We had to drag her the full distance on only one occasion. On two subsequent occasions, we dragged her a short distance before she agreed to rise and walk into the program.

We eventually decided to exert increased force and control, so we placed her in the induced swimming situation. She quickly adapted to her own style of bobbing and keeping afloat. The extreme control that the instructor-therapist exerted quickly established a "child-significant fig-ure" relationship in the Sullivanian sense. That is, Susan was so depend-ent on the therapist for her safety that nonverbal or verbal commands were quickly adhered to. Voicing a command was quickly conditioned to and the voice commands became more and more effective when Susan was active in other activities such as games, arts and crafts, rhythms and dance. When activated in this fashion, Susan appears to be happy and participating with others in the program.

On occasion we have been accused of using cruel or insensitive techni-ques. As therapists, we reviewed our value system and decided to take our stand with the following rationale: those persons waiting for spontaneous recovery are willing to wait indefinitely, with the result that the child is perpetuated in a state of exclusion from school and other groups and put into the back wards of state institutions such as Willowbrook. This state of affairs seems to us to be extremely cruel just as the continuous ravages of the inactive and disuse state, to begin with, are extremely cruel.

By use of our directive methods, we have achieved an increased func-tioning of these children physically, intellectually, individually or in groups, and in apparent happiness. There does not appear to have been any ultimate emotional damage to the children by virtue of our methods. Indeed, the children are, perhaps for the first time, receptive to the sort of love and affection which they need and which can help them to make progress. However, to prevent misuse or misinterpretation, we have con-stant reviews, seminars, and supervision of our staff. We have also been successful in keeping an increasing number of children in community-based day programs and out of State institutions.

If we are correct in our assumption that autonomy of action and ability to react and adapt to environment are basic to the development of func-tionally impaired children, then we feel our techniques should be utilized to elicit these responses until some other means of motivating and induc-ing purposive activity can be found. Our methods have proven quite successful in integrating and crystallizing the ability of the children to behave autonomously and to join into group activity. The ability of the children to respond to the commands and desires of other individuals also is enhanced, thus making their management easier and the ability to progress more likely.

CHAPTER XII

Therapeutic Recreation and Activity

Therapeutic recreation is beset by some doctrinaire concepts that remove recreation from its context in developmental science; therapy from its rehabilitative process; and confuses the needs of the ill and disabled with problems of integration as they apply to the issues of race and civil rights.

Recreation as a Developmental Concept

Fun is the ideal product of recreation but it cannot be attained without its development from activities that may or may not (at a given moment) have fun as their product. Fun is an end product of learning and experience. Its full attainment is rarely achieved in our culture.

According to Freud, an infant functions primarily on the pleasure principle. That is, the child remains inactive so long as all of its basic needs (food, elimination, warmth, etc.) are taken care of. It becomes active because of processes that can best be described as the reality principle: the infant is confronted with reality (absence of food, chilling, etc.) and cannot obtain help unless it acts on the environment by crying for assistance, kicking for warmth or to avoid irritation.

When random crying results in the mother offering the bottle or breast or the removal of wet-cold diapers, the infant begins to relate the activity process to the reattainment of pleasure. Schachtel adds to the primary and secondary process the observation that a normal infant tends to explore his environment. This exploration, says Schachtel, results in the attainment of new objects for satisfaction of pleasure. Ultimately the process of exploration itself becomes pleasurable (if not blocked) and is the essence of the creative process.

The child learning to stand pulls himself to the erect position in his crib hundreds of times and falls hundreds of times. At first each fall results in crying and expressions of fear. However, the continuous attempts result finally in successful standing. The child can be observed giggling and laughing as he finally attains the upright position sucessfully.

Games, in their initial phase, are related to the resolution of relationships between the child and his parents, his siblings, and later, his friends and peers.

The child strives in the beginning first to just play, then to win. He must best his father in some of the games so as to resolve some aspects of oedipus. He then challenges and tries to best his friends so as to feel that he can assert his ego over others and win parental favor and approval.

Later on he may try to excell in a sport. This requires grueling devotion to physical activity. It requires the overcoming of fatigue, pain, and blows to the ego when the game is lost. Even when winning, the victor at the end of the swim, for instance, is beset with nausea and exhaustion. The denial of pleasure can hardly be described as fun.

Therapy and Recreation

Therapy means treatment; that is, the utilization of specific or general processes that lead to amelioration of disease or disability. The random, nondirective exposure to recreative processes whose objective is fun cannot be termed therapeutic. A therapy must have the objective of ameliorating disease or disability with fun being secondary to its purpose.

Activity process and recreation afford a way through which activity in the handicapped can be developed and the various levels of development measured (in the social process, the actaivity process, the ego process, etc.). Recreation can be utilized for the amelioration of disease (emotional, physical, social) and disability. However, for these processes and techniques to be considered therapeutic, they must be directed and applicable to specific illnesses and handicaps.

A person sitting at a party and not participating in some way is not being treated. Let me discuss an entire disability area which will illustrate my point.

The Severely Involved and Profoundly Retarded

What Strauss terms catastrophic behavior seems to involve a person so completely that his response to stimuli of normal intensity is minimal. A person demonstrating such behavior seems to be unable to function as a member of a group. Other behaviors observed in brain-injured retarded children such as continuous thalamic crying or laughing, hyperactivity, and distractibility, seem to keep such children out of group fields for long periods of time. The consequence of these autistic events is exclusion from participation in the groups and from the possiblity of development in a field of minimal human interaction.

The frequent lack of bowel control and the uncontrolled impulsivity of brain-injured children can be viewed from this concept of minimal human interaction. The effect of bowel training by the parent and the developmental effect of peer relationships on group-approved individual behavior will be minimalized, if effective at all, in children who are out of the interactive field for long periods of time.

Another block to development of the brain-injured retarded child may be the lack of verbal interaction by the anticipation of need by a parent and the unidirectional character of verbal relations toward the child. The parent gives instructions to the child but the child cannot communciate or answer the parent. The ability of the child to initiate may atrophy as the parent shortcuts the need for problem-solving activity.

Ability to function in a group is epigenetic in nature. From early random movements and autistic behavior the infant begins to develop purposive movements, attention to and interaction with things and individuals in the external environment, and, finally, an ability to move toward others and to participate in groups. The brain-injured retarded child, in contrast, is often autistic for long periods of time and so does not involve himself in interactive situations. Many of these children are most often out of field and have not developed the faculty to make contact.

Many recreation programs and school programs try to interest these children in a permissive activity where little or no involvement is demanded; the rationale being that the child will be drawn into the group events by his own volition or by the group. Or he is isolated in a Strauss-like technique, where impinging stimuli are reduced and tasks presented to him. In either case, the interaction is unidirectional (imposed without having the child take over or initiate) and in many instances is minimally effective if effective at all.

The lack of faculty to make contact seems to be a function of the disorder itself. The degree of ability to make contact seems to be proportional to the degree of severity of the injury. In the brain-injured retarded, the degree of severity is often so great as to preclude contact for long periods and results in secondary disabilities—products of a lack of access to a contact with interactional events and persons. Intervention into the isolation of these children can affect the epigenetic development of skills, development of appropriate behavior, and the child's ability to interact with others and to be involved in group activity.

If a child is involved in a group activity, even without his volition, he begins to perform appropriately and, after several periods of involvement in the same type of activity, will tend to join that activity again at his own volition. For instance, in a round dance the child began to follow through in the activity required of the group. After a series of such involvements, the child joined subsequent activities of this type on his own and was able to participate in future and more complicated activities of the same sort. This technique has been used quite frequently in dance activities, which are part of "habilitation programs" of the Institutes of Applied Human Dynamics.

During recreation, a staff member of "habilitation programs" establishes a one-to-one relationship with a child. This staff member arranges the work area so that it is difficult for the child to escape from proximity to the work and the staff member. The staff member then moves the child's hands and tools through a purposive activity, such as hammering out a metal ash tray. The activity here may be described as analogous to Sister Kenny's methods in training polio-involved muscles at "Cerebral Zero." The staff member moves the hands of the child through the activity passively and, speaking to the child, attempts to have him take over the action. As the child begins to initiate and carry through the action, the staff member withdraws his direction of the activity. In this way, purposive movement has been developed in some brain-injured retarded children.

Another contact technique is used in swimming. In water, the child seems to be oblivious of all persons except the instructor and of all activities other than those of the instructor. If the instructor communicates a calm, nonanxious demeanor to the child (in a Sullivanian sense), then the child seems to interact on a nonverbal level. Contacts made during swimming seem to enhance staff-client interactions during other activities of the program as well. The child is conditioned to swim and is made to swim even without a willngness to do so.

The need to swim is reinforced by the aversive effect of sinking in the water when body movement is reduced. When the child can control his movements in water, his random actions are reduced and the water is no longer negatively reinforcing. Now the child is able to swim and enjoy it and the effects originally associated with sinking become extinct and are replaced by effects related to success. As participation in group and purposive activity is increased, there is a commensurate reduction in random activity and an increase in the control of body demands (such as bowel control).

Thus techniques for drawing an autistic child into interaction with others and into action and reaction to and with his environment have been developed. As stated earlier, this development seems to be epigenetic in character and a child seems to be able to involve himself in other interactive activities. Many brain-injured retarded children do not, of their own volition, become involved in interactive activity, and they need to be initiated into it by individuals who understand the dynamics involved.

In the above examples, we have demonstrated that mere exposure to a recreation atmosphere could not result in a therapeutic end. Severely involved, emotionally disturbed individuals and persons with severe involvement subsequent to stroke, trauma, etc. may also be found to be so distant from a level of awareness as to be excluded from recreation by nondirective techniques.

The Rehabilitative Process

From its very inception, rehabilitation has demonstrated that only a total attack on all aspects of a person's disability could result in a full reduction of that person's handicap. Treatment of a person in an isolated medical department, in an isolated physical department, in an isolated vocational setting, and in an insolated recreational setting does not fulfill the objective of rehabilitation. The integration of such needs can best be served in a setting where clinical leadership and experience can be exchanged at staff meetings and the client or patient can be observed in the treatment situations by all practitioners who serve him.

Segregation Versus Integration

If we integrate the ill, the disabled, and the handicapped into normative settings, we remove them from the therapeutic and rehabilitative milieu. We are, in effect, saying that such persons do not need a therapeutic milieu; they have gone about as far as they can go in the treatment milieu and the main objective now should be fun.

The disabled and handicapped (in their ever-changing needs at each age level, etc.) can best be served in a clinical setting, where they can have access to many rehabilitative services and where the recreation is therapeutic, that is, where it is addressed to the amelioration of the changing aspects of the disease or disability.

In recent years, programs for the handicapped have been moved to nontherapeutic settings. Clients are integrated into activities with normative groups. The borderline handicapped are often integrated. However, those with more severe problems are still placed in special groups, while those with severe stigmata are excluded from all of the settings collectively and the opportunity for expression in each setting.

These programs are addressed to accepting the handicapped as they are, but not mainly to the amelioration of the disease or disability. Amelioration may occur but not as a result of an effort by a professional to obtain it, thereby leaving amelioration to accident. Intervention allows for quicker change, improvement, and correction.

Treatment can be done only by persons trained in the rehabilitative and therapeutic process who have a knowledge of disability and who have benefit of clinical services, acting as a clinical team.

We must make a distinction between recreation for the handicapped and therapeutic recreation. A setting where there is recreation for the handicapped must first include a clinical team for its work to be rehabilitative; and its work must first be addressed to treatment rather than to fun for it to be therapeutic.

Just as all treatment is addressed toward bringing a person as close to normal as possible, therapeutic recreation aims to ameliorate disability so that a person can ultimately function in a normal setting, where possible, and have fun. At the point where the client is fully developed and the disability fully stabilized, the handicapped individual can benefit from a graduated integrated setting.

CHAPTER XIII

The Need for Personal Adjustment Training. A System of Behavior Modification

Foundations for P.A.T.: A Review of Research

According to the Office of Vocational Rehabilitation, Personal Adjustment Training is a vital part of a vocational rehabilitation program (DiMichael, 1950). In P.A.T., there is a sympathetic understanding of the personal adjustment needs of an individual and their importance for the total rehabilitation of the individual (Ibid.).

According to the Department of Vocational Rehabilitation Manual, P.A.T. may be provided for any one or any combination of the following reasons:

1. To aid the client to acquire personal habits, skills, and attitudes that will enable him/her to function effectively on the job despite the disability.
2. To develop or increase work tolerance.
3. To develop work habits and orient the individual to the work world.
4. To provide skills or techniques for the specific purpose of compensating for the loss of a member of the body or sensory function.

Rockower (1950) defines P.A.T. as a prevocational service of therapeutic value. It attempts to develop or strengthen fundamental qualities related to job adjustment which are commonly taken for granted. The retarded group, in particular, is lacking, for reasons other than lack of job skills, in a readiness to assume work responsibilities. Job readiness requires work motivation, proper work habits, regularity of attendance, and a maintenance of acceptable social relationships with others. The service of P.A.T. is of value particularly to persons with no previous work experience and who do not understand the overall demands of work. P.A.T. is provided in a rehabilitation workshop and ordinarily precedes occupational training or job placement.

DiMichael (Ibid.) thinks that objectives of P.A.T. are the development of caring for one's personal needs, development of an ability to travel alone, development of a knowledge of the skills of social interaction, and development of specific habits required in employment. These are such habits as promptness, neatness, ability to take supervision, ability to work under pressure, and ability to make a sustained effort to produce assigned work.

Jacobs and Weingold (1960) state that the most common training need presented by retardates is in the area of personal adjustment. They say that personal adjustment is a broad area covering not only the behaviors necessary for individual self-sufficiency but also the skills required in social interaction. There is a close relationship between social adjustment skills and behaviors and potential adjustment to a job, whether in sheltered employment or competitive employment. These writers go on to say that P.A.T. is commonly considered to be a prevocational service and preliminary to vocational training.

For many retardates, long periods of P.A.T. are often necessary because the retarded are so deficient in social skills, self-concept, and readiness to assume adult roles. P.A.T. becomes, in effect, equivalent to vocational training, for, even though the retarded person does not usually receive vocational training during or before P.A.T. because of his inability to learn specific trades, work ability is developed during P.A.T. The skills learned during the development of work ability may be of vocational value (Ibid.). These descriptions of Personal Adjustment Training programs and statements of the nature of P.A.T. are substantiated by related research.

In 1935, Bolton, of the University of Michigan, studied 75 mentally defective boys before they entered the Ford Trade School. The boys were all over 15 years of age and had less than a sixth grade academic ability (DiMichael, 1950). The boys were rated on school appraisal cards according to: Ability to work with others; ability to follow directions; academic ability; accuracy; attitude toward work; attitude toward criticism; deftness in handling material; shop courses completed; physical strength; personal appearance; regularity; responsibility; speed and energy; courtesy; trustworthiness; and power of self-expression.

Each rating had a numerical value: Excellent - 4; Good - 3; Fair - 2; Poor - 1. The highest possible score was 68 (17 characteristics x 4 *= 68). Eighty percent of those with scores over 45 proved successful in the Ford Trade School. The study showed that the most important traits, those which seemed to be the traits differentiating between successful and unsuccessful trade experience, were: ability to work with others, attitude toward criticism, deftness in handling material, regularity, personal appearance, courtesy, and trustworthiness.

Study of all the students in the school showed that the main reasons for failure in courses were the same for the boys with normal intelligence (normal on the basis of academic grades and I.Q. tests) and the retarded boys, namely: tampering with tools, disturbing others, chronic absence, tardiness, and unwillingness to continue training. *This tended to indicate that failure was a matter of adjustment and not of intelligence or work skills.*

Potts (1950), in summarizing a study of the past experience of the Michigan Office of Vocational Rehabilitation, reports that above a certain mental level, personal adjustment ability is a greater determinent than I.Q. rating in predicting success on a job.

Adjustment failures most often seem to be the result of poor home background and social and economic disintegration. A mentally deficient person who is industrious and has a stable personality can become self-supporting (provided, of course, that his intelligence is not extremely low).

Socialization is an important factor in the client's employability. Cohen (1961) studied 450 students entering Johnson Center, Bordentown, New Jersey, who had been given job opportunities. He found that about one-third failed because of poor adjustment to the community.

The Need for P.A.T.: A Review of Research

Lythe (1961) says: State DVR's buy services from sheltered workshops. Many state directors are not sure what they are getting when they purchase evaluation, personal adjustment, or vocational training programs for their clients. Somewhere, some certification is needed as to what is an adequate service so as to guarantee that the service rendered is worth the money spent.

The need for P.A.T. and the basic philosophy and objectives of P.A.T. have been stated by the Vocational Rehabilitation Administration (V.R.A.), the Office of Vocational Rehabilitation (O.V.R.), and experts and researchers in the field. Prior to this review and the *Handbook* that follows at the end of this section, literature on P.A.T. was scarce. No standard reference book on this vital area of habilitation and rehabilitation was available to persons in the field.

Adjustment Training and the World of Work

Young (1940) says that adjustment training should include intellectual and academic training; training in work skills and techniques; training in moral values; training in health and safety; discipline; respect for authority.

In our society, adulthood and self-support, usually through work, are synonymous. This is becoming increasingly true for women as well as for men. Landis (1947) states that no person is fully mature until he can earn his own way and be free of parental control. Young (1940) considers work a symbol of maturity, a medium by which persons can make contact with others, and a basis for status and prestige.

Hoppock (1957) says that work affords recognition and approbation; interpersonal relationships; affection; opportunity for mastery and achievement; opportunity for exercising the need to help others; opportunity for social-economic status; opportunity for development of moral value schemes; opportunity for satisfying dependency needs and for being directed by others; opportunity for achieving economic security and independence.

Young (1940) states that in our culture when persons are unemployed and/or lack work opportunity for a considerable length of time, there is often a loss of a sense of security; the development of a sense of inferiority and guilt for not contributing to family and community; the development of aggressive attitudes; a loss of courage, ambition, and morale; frequent retreats (sojourns) into fantasy; escape into illness; and criminality based on money needs.

Work requires conformance to standard rules of procedure and techniques of handling things and a focus of attention away from the subjective world of an individual. There is both direct and indirect interaction with others in the world of work. Work brings about physical and social contact of workers with other workers. Work requires that a person identify with the nature of work and with wages. There must be a regularity of work habits. Young states further that work habits are based on the need for regular hours of work; the repetitive nature of work; the need for routine motor habits which, once learned, should be kept alive by practice; the concept of a specific work space; and predetermined monetary returns.

For some types of work, a person must work rapidly for a period of time; have adequate strength in hands, arms, legs, and back; have adequate finger dexterity and hand, arm, and leg movement; have proper hand-eye coordination, foot-hand-eye coordination, and coordination of both hands; and have an ability to move both hands independently.

Work often requires that a workers estimate the size, quantity, and quality of objects. There must also be a perception of form and an ability to estimate the speed of moving objects (Baer, 1951).

In addition to the above Baer also includes the following: propriocentive discrimination; memory for things; abstract memory; ability to remember directions; general intelligence; ability to adapt to changes; ability to make decisions, ability to plan; initiative; an understanding of mechanical devices; attention to many things; oral expressiveness; ability to deal with people; memory for names and persons; grooming; ability to concentrate amidst distractions; emotional stability; ability to work under hazardous conditions; ability to work under unpleasant physical conditions; ability to judge height and weight.

Delp (1957) states that a person should have an attitude towards daily work activities which will bring about such intangible job results as accuracy, consistency, and attention to duties.

Landis (1947) adds to the list of characteristics of an ideal worker, an ability to travel from home and local neighborhood to work areas (job) and the ability to leave friends and associates to go to work.

With respect to postschool preparation for jobs, DiMichael states that both the deferred placeable group and the sheltered employable group of retarded adults can benefit vocationally from a range of services, including personal adjustment training (Mackie, 1959).

According to the National Committee on Sheltered Workshops and Homebound Programs, state vocational agencies should determine through a vocational diagnostic method if a client needs personal adjustment services before he is given training for a particular vocation or is placed on a job (*Handbook*, 1952).

Hamilton (1950) states that P.A.T. should include improvement of muscle tone and coordination. In addition, P.A.T. should develop a better understanding of the demands of the work world and of the nature of occupations, especially if the client has never before had paid employment. Hamilton states; "The actual activities followed may be immediately or only remotely related to the employment objective."

Potts (1950) thinks that some evening programs, although connected only remotely to work, have a positive effect on a client's ability to work.

Adjusting to the Work World: A Developmental View

A child's development depends to a great extent on its contact with adults and with other children (Wortis, 1950). Children identify themselves with each other and learn attitudes toward work and authority from each other (Young, 1940). This identification is highly important because it means that new patterns, other than those of the family, emerge and serve to widen a person's outlook and activities. This prepares a person for adult life. One who is placed in a restricted social group will have imprinted indelibly the pattern of this group, while one who has contact with many groups will acquire a diversified pattern. Though this may cause problems as to just what group the person belongs, it does aid in enabling the individual to adjust to different situations.

Personality and adjustment are made and marred by experience. The social group has the power to build attitudes and habits that will constitute the basis for an individual's social behavior, according to Landis (1947). Skills in behavioral adjustment are as important as mechanical and vocational skills and the media in which they are generated are often based on the scope and range of the group to which an individual has access. Access to work and work itself are intimately related to the adjustment or maladjustment of an individual.

Wortis (1950) states that work has exceptional significance for adjustment because it gives an individual an opportunity to preserve and strengthen his power of awareness and to maintain contact with the external world. In fact, if the work performed is meaningful and constructively contributory, skill not previously present (i.e., latent and not developed) in an individual may develop in the course of a work activity. Therefore, according to Wortis a P.A.T. program must use work itself as a core for the development of adjustment.

Adjustment to Work: Importance of Physical Factors

Adjustment and maladjustment are also dependent upon physical factors. In order to evolve successfully from everyday situations, a person should be in the best possible physical condition. Therefore, it is important to eliminate defects or reduce their effect on a person's actions, if either is possible (Delp, 1957).

When a person has acquired a regular and consistent routine in the care of his basic physical needs, he has provided for the predication and control of his future needs. If an individual has a set of stable habits for handling physical needs or wishes, he will react in a stable and predictable manner in later situations (Young, 1940).

Baer (1951) has developed a physical demands form for employment adjustment:

1. Working speed	14. Carrying
2. Depth perception	15. Sitting
3. Color vision	16. Reaching
4. Seeing	17. Kneeling
5. Hearing	18. Crouching
6. Talking	19. Stooping
7. Feeling	20. Turning
8. Fingering	21. Standing
9. Handling	22. Climbing
10. Pulling	23. Balancing
11. Pushing	24. Running
12. Throwing	25. Jumping
13. Lifting	26. Walking

Work Adjustment and the Home Environment

Young (1940) states that the adjusted worker is one whose feelings of adjustment are related to feelings of success, which are in turn related to job efficiency, ego satisfaction, and a useful role in society. On the other hand, the maladjusted worker is so intellectually and emotionally maladapted to his work and society that he is unreasonably irritable, unhappy, and morose. He is likely to drift from job to job, either because of external pressure (employer) or internal pressure (conflicts of adequacy). His feelings grow from the experience of failure.

In our culture, failure is related to the gaining of status, and failure to gain status leads to a sense of inferiority (Landis, 1947).

Inferiority feelings evoke feelings of being inefficient and ineffective. The compensations for feelings of inferiority are anger, aggression, overcompensaton, withdrawal, or fantasy and withdrawal by fears and anxiety (Young, 1940).

Abel and Kinder (1942) found in their study of subnormal adolescent girls placed on jobs that failure in fourteen cases could be attributed to unfavorable home situations. The failure could be related either to rejecting and dominating parents or to the piling on of responsibilities beyond the capacities of the girls involved.

Maladjustment can almost always be traced back to the home situation. Of course, virtually all psychological traits can be traced back to the home because the average individual spends at least half his waking hours in the home. Nevertheless, it is of significance that some maladjustments are cause by the parents' inability or lack of desire to return a child's affection warmly or to initiate affection. Indifferent or rejecting parents develop in a child a feeling of insecurity which he is frequently unable to completely overcome in later years. On the other hand, children who are overprotected may have difficulty in taking care of themselves later on. Parents who are anxious to compensate for their own feelings of inferiority are sometimes too anxious about their children's achievements. They may try to force the child to do things that he is incapable of doing. Parents whose self-images have never been achieved or whose mastery of occupational goals have been thwarted are likely to overregulate their children's lives. This often prevents the child's development of responsibility.

Parental Attitudes

Three attitudes (other than a suitable reaction) are often observed in the parents of handicapped children: resentment of the burden, overprotection, and outright rejection. Many behavior problems in the handicapped child arise as a reaction to these parental attitudes. The parent's unsolved problems often determine their attitude towards a handicapped child. (For practical purposes, a suitable reaction may be considered as an avoidance of resentment, overprotection and rejection. Casework with the family may be necessary in connection with a client-trainee in a sheltered workshop.)

The oversolicitude of parents of handicapped children is often attributed to their feelings of guilt for the occurrence of the disability and to the concept that moral outlook may affect the workings of the physical world. Often seen is a mother who considers the disability as a "cross to bear." To conceal her negative attitude toward the child, she demonstrates some anxiety concerning its welfare and exaggerates the duty of being a good mother.

Sometimes the child is openly resented. The mother is aware of her hostile feelings but builds up defenses to justify them. She blames society for its prejudices against the disability. She blames the doctor, the teacher, and others who deal with the child. She blames the world at large—with its "atom bombs and radiation causing deformities," etc.—for her troubles, and thinks that perhaps consumption of alcohol or cigarettes during pregnancy or marriage outside her ethnic group was responsible for what happened.

There is little information on the number of divorces caused by a belief that dissoluton of the marital union is the only way to prevent a recurrence. However, Boles (1961) did study the attitudes of cerebral palsy children and did consider how the problems affected marriage and caused divorce.

An Example of a P.A.T. Program

There is very little material on P.A.T., whether in published, mimeographed, or limited-circulation printed form. The following, however, is an outline of a P.A.T. program, from material of the Westchester Chapter of the Associaton for Retarded Children.

General Concepts

The P.A.T. program is a three-phased operation which lasts for twenty-six weeks. The effecting of factors and concepts takes place by *orientation, identification,* and *function.*

Orientation. Concepts, activities and situations are explained to and discussed with the trainee.

Identification. The trainee reveals an understanding of the orientation by showing an ability to identify what is being discussed, either verbally or by pointing ot, and by demonstrating ability in a dry run.

Function. The trainee functions for a period of time according to the concept presented and applies the concept situationally. For example:

1. Orientation: the time clock is pointed out to the trainee and its operation and use are explained.

2. Identification: the trainee is then asked to explain, in his own words or actions, what the time clock is used for. He is asked to point out and to demonstrate that he has become oriented. He will be asked to go through a dry run to show his initial understanding of the operation of the time clock.

3. Function: the trainee is then observed to see if he retains his knowledge of the use of the time clock for a period of time, i.e., if he performs the punching in, punching out action at appropriate times every day.

The ability to use a time clock may seem, to an ordinary person, to be a minor accomplishment. For a retarded person, however, it is of major significance that he is able to demonstrate an understanding of what has been presented.

The A.R.C. Program

Introduction—Four Weeks

Week 1:   Topics are:
—staff members—introduction to them, who they are, where they are located, what they do, why they are there, how they do *their* jobs;
—time card and time clock—why and how we punch A.M. and P.M.;
—water fountain; lunchroom; where and how we wash up; sink; toilets; smoking areas; work areas; coffee, milk, soda and other refreshments—where located and when to take breaks for food;
—lunches—eating a good lunch, bringing own lunch or buying lunch; carfare.

Week 2:
—lateness; notifying someone when absent; health; eating breakfast before work; clean work clothes; holidays; attendance.

Weeks 3 and 4:
—travel to work; work situations; remaining on work and not leaving work to talk; working with others; kinds of jobs.

Safety Adjustment: On the Way to and from Work and on the Job—One Week

Week 5:
—safety and prevention of accidents; reporting accidents; safe clothes to wear at work; appropriate jewelry; avoiding shop accidents; alertness.

Practical Aspects of Work and Adjustment to Others—Four Weeks

Weeks 6 and 7:
—authority; supervisors and foremen—getting along with them; counselors;
—proper language; control of anger; shop setting.

Week 8:
—grooming for the job; making friends and keeping them; how to shave; how to put on cosmetics; use of bathroom; how to take care of clothes; how others expect you to look—friends, employer, family; locker; clothes to wear to work.

Week 9:
—what to do at break time; being reliable—what it means;
—being understood (concentration on speech or other means of communication, so that others will understand what is being said or communicated).

Social Adjustment—Two Weeks

Weeks 10 and 11:
—working with others; working alone; working facing others; working facing wall;
—sharing tools; sharing work; partners on a small task; the people in the shop as a group.

Overall Adjustment to Shop Situation—Two Weeks

Week 12:
—initiative; keeping busy—how and why to enjoy what is being done; finding something useful to do when work is slow; accuracy; doing good work.

Week 13:
—jobs we can do; jobs we can't do; jobs we can get; jobs we can't get.

During the next thirteen weeks, sophistication in the above concepts is developed through experience, aided by situational, personal, and group counseling.

The Diagnostic Use of Personal Adjustment Training in Work Activity Centers

Many of the standard tests are inadequate for dealing with the handicapped. This disability group often cannot verbalize or perform sufficiently well within the confines of test protocol. An opportunity to perform in a real-life situation, over a long period of time, is necessary to achieve more accurate diagnosis.

Training, as with diagnosis, cannot follow the ordinary procedure used with the adequately verbal population. All training techniques, such as behavioral modification, work experience, counseling, guidance, education, environmental manipulation, role manipulation, and family relationships must be employed.

Many public and private agencies use the Intelligence Quotient (I.Q.) as a screening tool for determining whether or not an individual can profit from rehabilitation services. Although I.Q. by itself is an indicator of total performance, *it is not adequate if there is a need to appraise more fully an individual's various strengths and weaknesses.* While a person may have an I.Q. within the range regarded as retarded, he may also have isolated skills. These can be utilized to compensate for other deficiencies. For example, a client may not have a high verbal ability but, if he is adequate in some performance areas, he may still be able to become a wage earner and participate in many social situations.

The United States Employment Service Test is not as verbal as many of the other standard tests. It is used to determine a work profile. Even this test, however, proves inadequate when the learning disabled, autistic, and some of the retarded are considered. These clients were not able to repond to enough material for the test to yield a profile, yet many of these same people are now employed.

Many other aptitude and achievement tests are inadequate for testing the mentally handicapped. They are not designed to elicit sufficient content form, or tap the skills of such individuals. An exception seems to be the projective tests. These can test those individuals capable of minimal performance. This criterion still excludes multihandicapped or severely limited individuals. They require still other methods of testing in order to elicit the same conclusions reached by projective test methods.

Finally, the one-to-one interviews, which are highly verbal, can sometimes give misleading impressions. Many counselors can cite interviews during which a client was able to verbalize. Yet, he voiced aspirations and skills which approximated fantasy. Some clients have verbalized a willingness to work and have claimed various skills; but in a performance situation, they did not demonstrate either the quality of willingness to work or the skill levels claimed.

In order to supplement the tests, it is necessary to bring in new information, beyond the scope of test determinations. *There must be a situational (functional) approach, which evolves from activity evaluation and training techniques.* A P.A.T. program, by nature and design, places emphasis on functional and action evaluation and training of its clients.

A Broad Proposal for a P.A.T. Program

A client, when admitted to the sheltered workshop, is oriented to the physical setup of the workshop and the routines of the workshop day. He is introduced to his co-workers and the staff, assigned a locker, and given a time card and work sheet. He is immediately introduced to an area of activity.

After this brief introduction to the workshop, the individual is observed to see how well he carries out instructions, follows routines, and performs tasks. Minimal instruction is given during this period. Efforts are made to determine the client's motivation; ability to perform; powers of retention; social skills; reaction to emotion-packed situations, such as supervision, competition, and responsibility; and work tolerance.

Following this initial period, the situation is structured and manipulated in order to determine the client's learning ability and if there is any potential for improved social and emotional behavior. This is accomplished by having the client perform in various work settings and in different fields.

The client works together with a large group; singly, in a large group; together, in a small group; singly, in a small group; and alone. He also works closely with members of the opposite sex.

He is also exposed to the following fields of work: food service, factory, porter, laundry, clerical, car wash, maintenance, etc. In each of these settings, his *role* is also manipulated. He is given an opportunity to work as an employee, on the lowest rung of the ladder. He is also tried in a quasi-supervisory role.

Taking into account observations by members of the staff, the client's family, and the client's peers, a training plan for the client is worked out at a clinical conference. Now the focus changes from evaluation to training. Emphasis is placed on improving assets and overcoming weaknesses. This takes place in all areas; medical, social, vocational, and psychological. *The workday becomes an active training situation,* in which all training techniques are used. On-the-spot (situational) counseling is provided whenever the need arises, instead of waiting for a scheduled counseling session. This proves most effective because the experience is still fresh in the client's mind. The event is reviewed, errors are pointed out, and corrective measures are discussed with the client and his immediate supervisor.

If the client is frustrated by a task, he is given instructions as to its correct performance. If he behaves inappropriately towards his supervisor or his peers, whether male or female, he is given immediate guidance.

When these measures do not bring about appropriate responses, the need for a change in his environment is indicated. The individual may be put into a new grouping, doing the same task, or he may be put into an entirely different area more commensurate with his abilities. This may involve working alone with the same or a different task. An individual who feels uncomfortable with people may be able to perform more productively in isolation.

When a task is too difficult and beyond the frustration tolerance of the individual, a different task is assigned, one less demanding than the first. The level of difficulty of the task is raised as tolerance increases. If a client exhibits an ability to accept the responsibility of a quasi-supervisory role, he is given a job in which he can demonstrate his sklls in organization, getting along with people on a nonpeer relationship, and in accepting responsibility. Some clients cannot sustain the pressures of this kind of role. They are placed into a less demanding situation, where they can continue to function on the job.

When it is necessary to strengthen the client's ability to sustain pressure, the individual is put into a role where all his strengths and skills are utilized. In addition to this manipulation, there is supportive counseling. This helps to create a more acceptable self-image. Controls are instituted so that, when his self-image becomes more realistic, his role can be changed to a more appropriate level for this stage of development.

There is an opportunity, by having a co-ed work situation, to observe an individual and educate him for appropriate behavior towards members of the opposite sex. Many institutionalized individuals have been deprived of these opportunities. They demonstrate a complete absence of controls in many social situations and require continued guidance over a period of time. As awareness of social behavior grows in the client, the discrepancy between his behavior and the desired behavior can damage the client to the extent that it distorts his self-image. He sees himself as opposed to and unable to cope with normal cultural patterns. It is here that the therapist must be doubly careful and supporting, so that the individual can develop in this emotionally-charged area with a minimum of setbacks.

Training in activities of daily living, as well as physical therapy to increase motor performance, is given to the individual so that he can cope with some of the demands placed upon him in growing towards self-sufficiency. Emphasis is placed on dress, cleanliness, the social amenities, personal development and growth, etc. All of these have the effect of building acceptance.

Vocational guidance is given during all of the various activities associated with work. If an appropriate job is available and the individual is ready to produce at a competitive level, he is advanced to a preplacement stage. He is made familiar with various types of jobs, their demands, and ways to find employment. A client who is placed in employment does not lose contact with the workshop situation. He is given support on the job and, if necessary, additional specific vocational training. This enables him to secure his position more firmly. Job follow-up is continued until it becomes evident that it is no longer necessary.

To make certain that placement does not leave the individual isolated, he is still involved in the social and recreational programs of the workshop. This provides an anchor for him until he is able to develop similar relationships in the outside community. Recreation is an ongoing part of activities during P.A.T., and one of the purposes of such a program is to maintan the continuity with the activity that goes on in the workshop.

Also, within a recreation environment there is still another opportunity for development. Those individuals who have similar likes and abilities tend to gravitate together. Competitive games are organized on an individual basis if the participants have enough ego strength to tolerate this kind of activity. Some clients are unable, individually, to sustain loss in competition. But when this is done in group games, the loss is not felt so keenly.

In summary, P.A.T. attempts to parallel those activities that the average person comes to participate in as he or she reaches adulthood: work, recreation, learning, and growth. It prepared clients for the competitive world yet gives them a base to return to when necessary. And it provides the more sheltered atmosphere that may be needed by those who cannot enter a competitive market, maintaining and enhancing their skills and growth as they assume a place in the world that possesses productivity, dignity, and value.

CHAPTER XIV

Programming of the Multihandicapped In a Work Activity Center

(by James Meyer, B.S.)

There exists today a dilemma that the years have done little to mediate or solve: how best to serve multihandicapped adults in the community. Most workshops for the handicapped are geared towards the higher functioning individual. He or she usually functions at a moderate to mild level of retardation and is able to be fairly productive in terms of work produced. Such a client also tends to be more passive, in contrast to those individuals who exhibit catastrophic or acting-out behaviors. Often, workshops will not accept these "problem" cases or, having done so, discharge them when the aberrant behavior becomes apparent.

At the Institutes for Applied Human Dynamics, our approach is toward those very individuals who have been refused or discharged from ordinary workshops. It is our feeling, our basic philosophy, that these individuals can and must be served.

Our methods and techniques for handling these clients involves the assessment of each client's needs. It is always understood by the staff that no matter the degree of acting out or level of functioning, it is part of the *nature of the disability for that client*. Such behavior or poor functioning is assumed to be the probable result of disuse, inactivity, and lack of behavioral modification that has existed until now. So often the acting out and hyperactivity obscure the true potential and level of functioning of the client. Only when these behaviors are faced and modified can valid indications of a client's functional level be found.

In the workshop, the best way of achieving desired results is to employ a therapeutic milieu—an environment where the atmosphere is conducive to a work situation. The client discovers, when he enters the workshop, that the staff demands a certain type of behavior. They are ready to help him attain a level of achievement and functioning that will enable him to be a better adjusted, more productive, and happy human being.

The following pages discuss some of our clients and will perhaps render a more vivid picture of people, staff, and techniques that are involved in the work of the Institutes.

Carlos. At first, Carlos would not even enter the workshop building. The staff decided the best method of dealing with him would be a directive one. He was told that he had better come inside, as the staff would not tolerate this sort of behavior. Using role-playing and psychodrama, the staff assumed the role of "the Boss" or "the Authority," in a real context of "the Job."

Carlos realized that he would not get his way by his obstinacy and that he was not, after all, going to be able to go home to his mother. He came in and sat down to work.

Today, Carlos is a trucker's helper in his community.

Carlos' story is rare in the case of the multihandicapped, in terms of his ultimate success. But, in the very beginning of his workshop experience, the staff perceived his behavior as part of his disability, not outside it. Our approach was directive and to the point. He, Carlos, was going to work. It was a new expectancy for Carlos, a realizable one, and the staff demanded his adherence to it. Previously, Carlos had either been denied admission or dismissed from workshop programs because of his resistance and acting out. While most multiply handicapped have disabilities too involved for them to ever belong to the competitive world, Carlos made it. The staff's demands were also a form of belief in him and his abilities.

In some cases, as in Carlos', a generalization effect occurs when a client attends the workshop. He or she may observe that certain behaviors are expected while others are not tolerated. In Carlos' case, role-taking in a directive way was used. He was not allowed to act out but neither would he be discharged from the program for doing so. To release him home would only reinforce his old behavior and probably increase its occurrence. In time, Carlos realized that the staff was not to be thwarted.

As the staff assumes various roles in the course of treatment, the clients come to respect them and respond to their authority. Finally, they realize that greater self-satisfaction results from acceptance of this authority and the rewards that ensue from an increased level of functioning and acceptability.

Another technique used at the workshop is operant behavior modification. The client produces the demanded response and is rewarded. Often, in the case of the multihandicapped, however, we cannot wait long enough for the desired response to appear. Disability may be so severe that the modification process is interrupted. When such a problem arises, the staff employs passive-assistance. A staff member may actually take the client through the physical motions of the desired act. After awhile, the client may develop the ability to work semi-autonomously. For him, this is a giant step away from isolation and uselessness. Were he allowed to sit idle until, by some unimaginable power, he began to perform the actions needed, he would probably regress even further.

Richard. This client was often very hyperactive. In order to modify his behavior, the nature of his workday was manipulated. Richard alternated between bench tasks and jobs requiring ambulation. He had shown episodes of distrust and disruptive behavior at the workshop as well as at his residential facility. The staff realized that his acting out was his way of "blowing off steam." By alternating sitting and walking, Richard began to change for the better.

Specifically, when Richard appeared ready "to blow," he was sent to work involving shipping and receiving. When he began to appear fatigued from this, he was again placed at his workbench. Once this format became a behavioral pattern, Richard was far more comfortable and productive.

Richard, when he first came to the workshop, had spent over twenty years in a state school. He had just recently been relocated in the community.

At the Institutes, clients like Richard—the disruptive and hyperactive—are assessed and their programs devised with those behaviors in mind. Every attempt is made to utilize the very behavior that once excluded such individuals from treatment.

Many clients, on the other hand, are fairly random by nature. When given tasks requiring ambulation, they tend to become even more random and disoriented. Again, the staff considers how best to use this individual's disability to determine what he can eventually be most successful in performing. Such is the case with Eddie...

Eddie. It was observed that Eddie became more random and hyperactive after he spent time loading and unloading trucks. He became tense and nondirected. When this seemed about to happen, he was placed back at his table. By working for a period of time at more structured tasks, a sense of tranquillity and control was provided that Eddie very much needed.

Many of our clients are confined to wheelchairs and are limited to table-related tasks. For these clients, it is important to provide a frequent change in the type of work assigned. This prevents habituation, which can lead to regression and increased acting out behavior.

We have found that the most important behavioral modification tool is the work itself. A client engaged in production goes through many changes. While in the beginning days at the workshop he may be resistive, fearful, aggressive or completely reject any assignments, eventually the repetition of the work and the demands of the staff provide a framework for his day. Those who are severely involved may come to incorporate the task into their behavior. The withdrawn or detached gradually reach increased levels of awareness and affect. They appear to follow directions better and interact with their environment, the staff, and other clients to a much greater degree. The hyperactive and acting-out client can now channel his energy into productive behaviors. In time, all our clients begin to function more effectively on every level of behavior. They achieve a new peace within themselves as self-esteem and self-satisfaction begin to emerge.

As the client becomes more productive, positive reinforcement increases. Should he regress, however, the directive approach is used. Money is a valuable positive reinforcer for the higher functioning. They are also aware that negative or tantrum behavior decreases their productivity and, consequently, the amount of money earned. For the lower functioning individual, merely receiving a pay envelope at the week's end is reinforcing. Even cookies and candy can be used, if necessary, to enhance good behavior.

Activity enables all clients to reach a higher level of functioning. Contract work in large volumes provides such an opportunity for productive work. These jobs present problems in fine and gross motor coordination, eye-hand coordination, perception, etc. They also offer a wide range of skills to be learned and incorporated as the individual changes and grows.

The clients we have discussed above are only a few of the many profoundly involved individuals with whom we work, aand the techniques described represent a small sampling of the methods we have used successfully. But this small overview serves to underscore the central theme found in all of our work with these clients: all children and/or adults can be worked with and stimulated. *No matter what degree of disablity or handicap, a certain level of growth can occur. To leave these individuals to idleness and disuse will, most certainly, bring out regression and further disability.*

Our technique is to discover and employ a specific set of conditions for each client that will promote his growth. Activity and stimulation, in varying degrees, will bring about this desired end.

Our philosophy, in all our work with the severely handicapped, is that all people are entitled to an authentic chance at life.

CHAPTER XV

A HANDBOOK
FOR
PERSONAL ADJUSTMENT TRAINING

By

Jack M. Gootzeit, Ed.D.

CHAPTER ONE

Introduction

Personal Adjustment Training (P.A.T.) is a technique used to bring about a therapeutic effect by controlling social relationships and physical environment. Evaluaton is made by observing the individual's reaction to physical environment, peers, authority, job, and self. Training is effected by manipulating tne environment and by moving the individual within a physical setting and within the social structure of a situation, in addition to instruction and counseling.

The *Handbook* explains the various aspects of Personal Adjustment Training to assist personnel who administer P.A.T. programs in techniques of handling their clients.

All specialized shops serving the multihandicapped have programs entitled "Personal Adjustment Training." However, in spite of the development of programs entitled P.A.T., there is little literature on the subject. Before this study, no specific study of P.A.T. existed, and there was no standard reference book on P.A.T.

The related literature (what little there is) on Personal Adjustment Training and, to some extent, the literature on adjustment; the investigator's experience in the field; and the results of a survey of thirty-seven shops specializing in services to the mentally retarded (from all geographic sections of the United States and the District of Columbia) were drawn upon to present the following:

—physical adjustment to work;
—work habits and adjustment to work;
—personal and interpersonal factors and concepts related to work;
—staff competencies: educational levels, professions;
—setting;
—techniques for P.A.T.;
—a proposed program.

Overall use of techniques presented in the *Handbook* came from the results of the survey and from the investigator's experience. Specific details of techniques had, of necessity, to come mainly from the investigator's experience and from the investigator's field observations of four selected workshops as part of the study.

In P.A.T., an attempt is made to answer such questions as: In a job situation, can the person being considered organize his work? Can he find solutions to difficulties?

As evidence is accumulated from situational observation, it is analyzed and a plan for manipulating the environment or situation is devised, using the results of observational evaluation and formal tests. The plan must be flexible because evaluation and training are not mutually exclusive.

In the workshop many clients, for the first time in their lives, are given an opportunity to be themselves. This opportunity to develop their own individual personalities, aided by Personal Adjustment Training, enables them to develop physically and socially.

It has been observed that, in the initial phase of participation in the program, many clients isolate themselves until they lose their fear of adults and authority. After this initial period of isolation, integration with their peer group and adults and supervisory personnel follows in stages. As they become aware of the accepting and supportive environment, they may relate first either to members of their peer group or to supervisory personnel. First relationships within their peer group usually develop with members of their own sex. Then, with acceptance, they relate to all the members of the group. Motor skills and coordination begin to change from gross to more precise. Manipulation of the environment is often sufficient to alter the factors which, heretofore, stunted the individual's growth emotionally, socially, and physically. The individual moves from one physical setting to another. He changes work settings and work groups within the shop. This movement may cause a change in social status, which may cause a change in demands placed upon him. Various physical settings may induce different reactions to the same type of stimuli, and different settings will be new stimuli themselves.

The learning of skills, both vocational and social, the developing of emotional control, and the engaging in new activities all help to bring the client to a higher plane of performance and behavior. Counseling, role-playing, group therapy, corrective physical exercise, and vocational training all play an important part in bringing about this improvement. Knowledge of different types of skills fortifies the client against regression.

Since P.A.T. takes place within the setting of work and the workday, it is quite obvious that there is ample opportunity for lengthy observation and training. Progress can be noted from day to day. Negative factors can be counteracted immediately.

Goals of Training

If the multihandicapped person can become an adequate worker within the family group, it can be said that he is self-supporting, even though he or she receives no wages. For example, a handicapped daughter for whom no vocational goal is in sight can become a homeworker and contribute to the efficient functioning of the family group. In the overall concept, it is the intention to plan for this type of rehabilitation if it is determined that it would be the most feasible solution for the client at the time of the initial P.A.T. contact.

If the multihandicapped individual is able to be prepared for a job, the preparation must be careful. The handicapped adult faces an unfamiliar world when he faces getting a job and sustaining himself on the job. This new environment will be in sharp contrast to the former environment where the retarded individual had no obligations, standards, or demands to meet. Behavior in accordance with the former type of world may have become ingrained:

On seeking a vocation, the person will move from a protected and somewhat asocial environment into a competitive and changing world. Leaving an environment of what may have been great solicitude from doting parents or family, he must now strive to attain the basic necessitites of life and the satisfaction of his need for maturity, reward, recognition, and self-realization.

In training, the handicapped adult acquires not only manipulative skills but also a pride in high-grade performance which enables him to get a "lift" out of doing a job well. Training attempts to develop the trainee to the point where a day's work becomes more enjoyable than the nondirective, nonobjective, asocial life he led formerly.

To adjust gradually to the work situation within the shop requires training in:

1. Self-care, grooming, personal hygiene, getting to work, time factors, proper eating habits.
2. Communication with supervisors, other workers, etc.
3. Acceptable interpersonal relations with others in the shop.
4. Developing satisfactions from work and the monetary rewards that come from productivity.
5. Development of realistic goals and aspirations.

The closer the individual comes to the norms of the real shop system, the greater his personal adjustment is to that system. Stopping short of these norms should be only as a result of true disability and not because of a handicap.

A handicap is a deviation that holds the individual back from his minimal adjustment to the shop. To the degree that an individual overcomes his handicap will that individual start on a more equal footing with other workers. It must be borne in mind that work does not satisfy immediate needs. There are social standards, rules, and techniques of handling materials to which all workers must conform. When a worker manipulates a piece of stock, he is engaged in a social act which brings him into contact with other workers and other workers into contact with him. These contacts develop within the trainee material identification, interest in wages, and identification of self and others as workers and as handlers of goods and stock. The worker also adjusts to duties of a repetitive nature that are taking place in a specific locale of a specific working space in a given and rigid regularity of time.

Training for the handicapped adult becomes an essential need directed toward the satisfaction of the demands of the shop system. This training is directed toward specific objectives which are always the attainment of some well-defined end: changing attitudes; increasing production efficiency; increasing motor function and strength; elimination of asocial or antisocal drives; stimulation of and making possible sustained interest and effort in getting a job; enjoyment of the fruits of labor; development of knowledge that will enable the person to function as an ordinary worker; and development of willingness and skill for the cooperation demanded by the shop.

In training the individual to fit into the roles that he will play in the shop system, there must be an opportunity to meet the physical, social, emotional, and vocational needs of the trainee within the framework of shop pressure.

The needs of production and the interpersonal relationships among workers, foremen, supervisors, directors, etc., help to form an environment in which adjustment to work and to the work situation can take place. Factors of maladjustment can be isolated in the work situation so that they may be remedied. A sheltered workshop provides a factory-type environment in which multihandicapped individuals above school age learn to develop personal, physical, social, and vocational skills. Because many of these individuals have never been in real work situations and because their disability is such that their learning processes are slower than normal, a longer period of concentrated training is needed to achieve satisfactory adjustment. Unlike most people who are in need of rehabilitation services and who have had prior work experience, this disability group needs to be exposed to and trained in a realistic work setting from the very beginning of their participation in a training program.

Methods of Training

The Personal Adjustment Training program affords an opportunity for problems to be analyzed and solutions given in a functional setting. An underlying assumption of P.A.T. is that function can be modified by training. The question arises, "How much modification is possible and to what extent will such modification assist a person to become employable?"

For those who attain the skills needed in competitive industry, selective job placement is the foremost goal. Sheltered employment is provided for those ready for placement but for whom no job has yet been found. For those who are not able to develop the necessary skills and make the necessary adjustments in the originally estimated period of time, sheltered workshop employment is available until the individual develops sufficiently to be considered ready for a job. The sheltered workshop, although not physically separate, is operated as a separate program.

Training, to be effective, must be applied during developmental phases. Instruction is primarily verbal and not written. If a client plateaus, the "waiting time" before a new developmental phase begins or a new training technique is developed is spent in sheltered employment. Training begins again when the client enters a personal phase when development is possible. Progress reports are kept on each client in a training program. Cases are reviewed periodically and professional conferences are held frequently, studying situations emerging from the work itself.

Family members are urged to participate in group meetings and individual conferences to discuss problems, including those arising from the client's being involved in the workshop program and those which need attention while the client is not in the shop but at home.

Prior to making a report to an agency, a clinic meeting of professional workers is held and the training plan is discussed. A meeting is held with the parents of the client and the findings are discussed. A follow-up clinic discussion is held. Suggestions from this discussion are included in the final reports and disposition plans.

Objectives of P.A.T.

1. To aid the client in acquiring job and personal habits, skills, and attitudes that will enable him to function effectively on a job in spite of being multiply handicapped.
2. To develop increased work tolerance.
3. To develop work habits and to orient the individual to the world associated with work.

4. To provide skills or techniques for the specific purpose of compensating for (or modifying) emotional problems, physical concomitants to brain dysfunction, and secondary social problems—all of which may interfere with a handicapped individual's adjustment to a job.

Definition of Personal Adjustment Training (P.A.T.)

Personal Adjustment Training (P.A.T.) is a process of instruction, training, and environmental manipulation practices in which an individual's pattern of work activity is fitted to those minimal standards of behavior demanded by the work world and the community.

Personal Adjustment Training programs fall into the following categories:

1. *Personal Adjustment Training—Work Experience.*
   A P.A.T. program which provides remunerative employment in a sheltered industrial or service work environmental setting, in which an individual's pattern of work activity is modified by access to work. Work supervisors and foremen provide work skill instruction and give the client an opportunity to develop skills at his own pace.

2. *Personal Adjustment Training—Situational*
   A P.A.T. program which provides remunerative employment in a sheltered environment such as described above, and under similar conditions. If and when problems arise in the course of work experience, rehabilitation counseling and casework is provided so that the client can maintain an optimum level of achievement and accomplishment on the job.

3. *Personal Adjustment Training—Rehabilitative.*
   A P.A.T. program providing remunerative employment, also in a sheltered industrial or service work setting. Here the individual's working pattern is analyzed and modified by the intervention of rehabilitation professionals who attempt to modify problems of an emotional, physical, or social nature in a work setting. If these problems require casework, extensive counseling, or physical rehabilitation services, these are provided by P.A.T. personnel or by cooperating agencies to which the client is referred.

The World of Work and P.A.T.

In the modern community, at the end of a suitable training period, a child must become self-sufficient to be considered an adult. In our society, high values are placed on a person's ability to work. It is considered to be a concrete symbol of maturity.

In order to be a wage earner, a worker must be productive enough to produce goods or provide services in such quantity and quality as to make it possible for an employer to pay wages (in addition to rent and overhead, etc.) and to make, in addition, a reasonable profit (the employer's wages). Most individuals have sufficient physical, personal, and interpersonal endowments and developed work habits to meet the demands of competitive industry and service work.

A handicap, however, by its very nature, often prevents individuals from acquiring the sklls and knowledge necessary to meet these demands through ordinary means. Because of this, special evaluation and training techniques are needed to determine the nature and extent of the inadequacy of adjustment to work and to bring a handicapped adult to maximum performance.

The experience of this investigator has tended to indicate that the handicaps of multihandicapped persons are so varied that each client must be analyzed individually. A program for adjustment must be tailored individually. However, there are at least three broad fields of adjustment:

1. *Physical Adjustment to Work*
   Problems the client may have include: sensory deficiencies; muscle weaknesses; balance, coordination, and dexterity deficiencies; all of which may affect employability.

2. *Work Habits*
   The client may not have minimal abilities to act in a typical manner demanded by work.

3. *Personal and Interpersonal Adjustment to Work*
   The client may not have those minimal standards of behavior demanded by other individuals with and for whom he works. These will need special attention.

Scope and Depth of the Handbook

The scope of the *Handbook* is comprehensive. The depth of presentation of techniques in the *Handbook,* however, is only so deep as is necessary for well-versed individuals to be able to use it as a guide for P.A.T. programs.

There are many minor details of technique for handling a particular problem. Because of this, extensive explanations of each and every technique as it applies to each and every possible situation in P.A.T. would produce an unwieldy book.

The method of presentation of this *Handbook,* therefore, will be to point out that certain techniques are used in certain situations. It is assumed that an individual competent in the field of the individual technique (counseling, physical therapy, casework, etc.) will know the minor details of the technique. For example, let us take the case of an individual who had difficulty in carding buttons.

The basic steps followed in carding buttons are:

1. The buttons are pushed through a card which has holes punched in it.

2. The buttons are then lined up on the card in such manner that the individual holes in the buttons line up with the holes in the card. A wire is passed through the holes in button and card.

3. After the wire has been passed through the holes in several rows of buttons, it is bent in such fashion that it secures the buttons to the card.

This series of actions requires, in the physical field, a degree of hand-eye coordination; a degree of finger oppositional coordination (to hold the buttons and the card); and degrees of wrist, elbow, and shoulder motions.

A foreman could handle this quite easily if all that was required was to show the task to the client and give him an opportunity, through work experience, to repeat the assigned task until he has managed to master it.

If, however, the client has difficulty in using his hand, i.e., has a general weakness or lack of coordination in his hand, a physical education instructor or a corrective physical educator might attack the problem by specifying that the client engage in games and repetitious exercises to strengthen the hand muscles until they are sufficient to perform the desired action. In games or exercise, the client might squeeze a ball, such as a softball, baseball, or a tennis ball.

If action is poor but a trace of muscle power is present, a physical therapist would use neuromuscular-reflex facilitation techniques to develop an ability to perform the desired action.

If the client is a cerebral palsied, retarded individual who has gross movement in the shoulder, elbow, and wrist, and who, because of disuse of muscles, cannot perform finger opposition sufficiently enough to hold a button or a card, a physical therapist can then initiate movement by the use of biometric reflexes. These are elicited when the client is placed hanging over a ball and is made to balance on hands and forearms; or the movement is developed to an initial functional level through neuromuscular facilitation techniques. At this point, an occupational therapist could give some craft activity which would bring finger opposition into play and would enhance the functional performance which the client demonstrated at a basic level.

In the case of a hemiparetic, neuromuscular facilitation techniques might consist of resisting flexion of the elbow in the functioning side. This will cause a reflex movement of the afflicted side, thereby eliciting initiation of subcortical movement beyond a trace.

If the individual can perform the desired action, it is important that he perform the action repeatedly. This repetition strengthens connections and muscles and also develops a work habit. At this point, the analysis of the situation moves from physical adjustment to work habits. Work hardening demands that the individual utilize the ability to perform the desired action in terms of time, speed, and productivity.

If the client can perform the action but does not have motivation to do so, the analysis of the situation moves into the personal-interpersonal, counseling area. The feelings of the client are elicited and counseling is used to assist the client in developing an incentive to perform the action.

"Division of Labor" Within P.A.T.

It was discovered from the survey that 102 professionals had a background in 21 different educational fields. As can be seen from the few, specific examples just given, a detailed discussion of each and every technique as it might apply to each possibility in the course of a P.A.T. program would entail producing a handbook for every professional and nonprofessional specialist involved in P.A.T..

A P.A.T. professional reading this handbook, however, could handle part of a situation if he were educated or had experience in a field related to an aspect of the situation. He could also ascertain what professionals would be able to handle those specific aspects which he was not qualified to handle himself. He might bring such a person into his workshop, or he might refer to an outside agency.

For example, a P.A.T. professional with a social work background might realize that he could handle the casework aspect of a particular problem, but that an occupational therapist was needed for another part of the problem. This "division of labor" in handling problems in P.A.T. arises from the necessity of having personnel with many and varied backgrounds for a comprehensive program. P.A.T. covers many aspects of adjustment. There should be competency on the part of the P.A.T. staff in all the fields covered.

CHAPTER TWO

**Physical Adjustment
To Work Coordination**

Coordination

Independent movement of both hands, hand-eye coordination, and foot-hand-eye coordination are the physical demands most often made of a worker. Coordination is a product of the growth and development of an individual and his access to activities which foster its development. Much of the poor coordination of the handicapped is believed to be a factor of brain dysfunction itself. However, in the investigator's experience, coordination can be advanced and adjusted to work-acceptable levels in a P.A.T. program.

Assessing Problems of Coordination

The problem of coordination may be graded as follows:

1. Coordination is below the level of workshop terminals (those persons who can work only in a sheltered environment).

2. Coordination is at the average level of workshop terminals and is suitable for workshop performance.

3. Coordination is more than suitable for workshop performance but detracts from client's employability.

4. Coordination is acceptable for employment.

P.A.T. affords a setting for evaluating and treating coordination problems functionally.

Methods of Modifying Coordination Problems

1. Coordination can be developed by a client's using skills on the job. If the job lasts for a period of time, the repetition of the same task can enhance further development of coordinaton.

2. Where coordination is severely impaired (as in ataxic or athetoid individuals), physical therapy and corrective exercises may make it possible for an individual to gain minimal abilities for work functioning. When a minimal level is attained through repetition, production work, aided by the motivation of this work and with pay as a positive reinforcer, can improve coordination function.

The Senses

The five basic senses—sight, including color vision, hearing, touch, taste and smell—are intimately involved in work demands. When these senses are impaired or impeded, the range of possible kinds of work that a person may do is narrowed. A blind person cannot be employed to match colored fabrics. A deaf person cannot be employed in testing sound qualities. And a person deficient in smell and taste ability would be of little value in cooking or food handling.

A P.A.T. program can assess a client's sensory deficiencies in relation to work. If these can be modified by medical intervention, the client can be referred to a doctor or medical agency. When medical intervention has modified the disability to the maximum, the P.A.T. program will provide an opportunity to assess the disability as it functionally modifies the client's ability to perform useful work. The client can be shifted from job to job to determine the kind of job he can do with maximal success.

Most vocational tests have difficulty in predicting success on the job. We have found the TOWER method of evaluaton deficient in this area and find, rather, that actual work in a work setting to be the best predictor of success on similar jobs elsewhere. Our basic line of reasoning in this area is as follows:

First, the client attains the highest possible level of physical function through medical intervention, etc. Then, through P.A.T., the client is trained to do the best with what he has, i.e., to work with his residual handicap—what is left as a handicap after corrective measures have been taken. We then test each client in actual work situations and record their ability to work and to use this work to gain skills and productivity.

Ability to Talk

Lack of ability to talk bars a worker from a wide range of jobs: telephone operator, salesperson, radio announcer, etc. However, being nonverbal does not impair an individual's ability to function significantly in a production or service industry.

The P.A.T. experience affords an opportunity to assess the functional limitations set by the client's inability to talk. It is possible to observe how this limitation actually interferes with the client's ability to function on a job.

Physical Demands of Work

Benchwork requires that a client sit for most of the time during an eight-hour day. Floorwork, service work, shipping, receiving, messenger service, and food service require that a worker spend long periods of time in standing and walking. Service and cleaning industries often require that employees be able to climb, run, and crawl (under things) in order to clean or repair equipment. Such abilities can be assessed while the client functions in a sheltered setting and can be developed by specific work assignments and in recreational programs. Other physical demands made by some jobs are an ability to do some work while kneeling, crouching, stooping, turning. If these abilities are impaired, access to work is impaired. Job opportunities will be limited because of an inability to perform such movements. A P.A.T. program can try to develop these capacities in broad recreation programs and work assignments. If these functional capacities are severely impaired, analysis and treatment by physical therapy and/or corrective exercise may be necessary.

Physical Skills

Work actions require gross neuromuscular skills such as balancing, handling, pushing, pulling, throwing, lifting, carrying and reaching; and fine neuromuscular skills, such as deftness, dexterity, fingering, and the use of finger opposition. The individual's abilities may be assessed from observation of job functioning. Moderate weaknesses are modified during work experience and exposure to work. Severe maladjustment requires the use of physical therapy and/or exercises of corrective nature.

P.A.T. can be used for the elimination or reduction of physical defects, for improvement of muscle tone and coordination, and for neuromuscular education and reeducation, particularly if a program of corrective physical exercise is included.

Work Judgment

Work experience, teaching, and instruction are the primary techniques for effecting physical adjustment. This is in contrast to counseling as a technique for effecting personal and interpersonal adjustment. These techniques can also be used to help develop such abilities as estimating size, shape, quality, depth, and speed. Work judgment—the actual application of such abilities to such tasks as noting differences between materials with respect to size and shape; or noting similarities between different things, etc.—can best be developed via work experience and occupational training.

Work Pace

An employer usually has minimal standards which demand certain levels of alertness on the part of his employees. These standards are usually based upon an employee's ability to keep pace with others and to maintain a common work speed.

In an actual job situation, there is usually a breaking-in period during which the employee increases speed as he becomes familiar with the functional task assigned him. However, it is expected that his breaking-in period will not last too long and that the expected level of productivity will soon be reached.

During P.A.T., a client's level of productivity, speed potentials, and motivations can be determined. Then, pay incentive, counseling, and group counseling can be used to make motivation more positive and to cause actual observable speed increases and improved productivity.

Fatigue

The standard workday in many fields is eight hours of work. The ability of a client to work for eight hours without undue fatigue can be developed by demanding a full workday of the client during the P.A.T. program. This conditions the client to full eight-hour workday demands.

A rehabilitation counselor can guide a client toward corrective after work activities, especially with respect to how much sleep the client should get every night. Presentation during classes and during orientation sessions of the causes of fatigue and necessary hours of sleep can also effect development of adjustment in this area by the client.

In short, work experience is the major technique used to develop an ability to endure the pressures of working for a living.

If the client cannot work a full day, job opportunities will be limited and sheltered employment may be the goal of training until such ability is developed.

Work Tolerance and Flexibility

A worker must often work in situations in which there are constant machine noises, loud talking, or loading sounds. In other work situations, a worker may be completely isolated. He may be called upon to function without contact with others. A worker must have the adequate ability to unlearn work skills as new skills and techniques are substituted for old ones. A worker must be able to shift from one assignment to another assignment at relatively short notice. This is done to avoid the development of work rigidity in a client in connection with specific work tasks. The worker must be able to develop new skills.

Counseling may be necessary if a sense of security arising from knowledge of how to perform a task, when compared in the worker's mind with the initial insecurity arising from lack of knowledge about the new task, impedes acceptance of the new assignment. The ability to be flexible is developed by exposing a client extensively to different work tasks. A rehabilitation counselor may assist the acceptance of different jobs and different work environments.

The development of "working hands" is sometimes part of industrial jobs and service activities. A realistic attitude towards blisters, calluses, minor muscular aches, etc., as part of the work situation must be developed. Am ability to remeber past events, and instructions, the location and appearance of material and tools, etc is necessary for a worker. He is also expected to plan and organize his work to some extent, and to develop his own sense of a work pace. Work organization ability can be developed through work experience.

For those who cannot develop basic physical skills, the sheltered workshop or work activity center affords work opportunity appropriate to each client's ability to contribute, at whatever level that may be. A client's ability to participate at even a very regressed level permits a release to his family for employment and other functions necessary for good family relations.

CHAPTER THREE

Work Habits and Adjustment to Work

Definition of Work Habits

We define a work habit as a disposition or tendency to function in a characteristic manner in relation to work. A constructive attitude toward work and the work situation should be developed so that the client will be accurate, consistent, and attentive in his job.

Attention to Duties, Attention Span, and Concentration on Work

Work requires a selective focus of attention on job essentials. Attention must be restricted to the task at hand and the worker must not take conscious note of stimuli which might be distracting. Such distracting stimuli might be: individuals in transit through the work area; the activities of others; accidental noises, etc.

An ability to sustain a focus of attention and an attention span can be developed. There is a relationship between the ability to sustain attention and the development of the cerebral cortex, the development of muscular controls, and the development of selectivity of focus of attention. Training in attention, therefore, may be both mental and physical.

How the client's needs will be met through work must be demonstrated to him. Pay, approbation, and pride generated by independence are some of the effects which will reinforce a constructive attitude toward work.

During a P.A.T. program, a client's ability to attend to duties can be assessed to determine if the client will be able to sustain a level of attention which would be satisfactory to an employer.

If the client's attention span is insufficient for work adjustment, the answers to the following questions must be found:

1. Is the cause physical, psychological, or social?

2. If it is physical:
   a. Can energizers (medically prescribed) assist in increasing an individual's ability to attend to duties? One characteristic of some retarded is that they appear to be not fully "awake." An energizer to activate them can sometimes solve the problem.
   b. Can therapeutic exercise improve muscle tone and facilitate neurological education? In our experience, we have found

that vigorous exercise, such as jogging or running in place for thirty minutes, often leads to increased activity and awareness.

c. Can attention be modified by decreasing fatigue factors and increasing endurance and ability to tolerate stress? We can physically condition the client so that he can produce the attention span required by a job.

3. If the cause of inattention is social or psychological, can it be modified in a physical setting?

Attention span can be increased by graded periods of work experience and work pressure. If muscular factors are related to inattention, general conditioning exercises specifically oriented toward increasing endurance and ability to sustain fatigue can be given during recreation periods or by a physical therapist, adaptive physical educator, child development worker, or therapeutic recreationist.

Incentives (goals) for attention span can be effected by increases in pay, demonstrations to the client that his production has increased, and the use of individual and group counseling as a situation evolves.

Consistency and the Repetitive Nature of Work

A producton industry or a service industry requires that a certain minimal quality of work be performed throughout the workday, the work week, and the work year. Most jobs require the development of a routine that must be adhered to consistently by an employee.

Consistency is developed during P.A.T. by developing concepts of time demands and an understanding of the routine repetitive nature of work. These concepts can be presented in group discussion and orientation sessions and can be reinforced situationally as the client demonstrates actual (physical) consistency on the job. When there is an indication that it is needed, individual or group counseling can be employed to further develop the concept of consistency as it affects each client in the world of work.

Regular Hours of Work

In our culture, most jobs are done during a specific time interval. During P.A.T., such concepts of work regularity as punching a time clock, punctuality, regular attendance, etc., can be devevloped. Work experience, pay-requisite awards for consistency, discussion and orientation sessions, group and individual counseling addressed to specific adherence to these concepts are all measures that can be used. Since work, in our culture, is usually based on a forty-hour week, this is an essential demand during P.A.T. It is modified only by the special needs of each client. (In some areas, a six-hour day or a seven-hour day is the rule and the P.A.T. program may be set up accordingly.)

Routine Motor Habits

As neuromuscular units are employed more and more in the successful performance of work, routine motor habits are developed and sustained, as long as the job remains essentially the same. Work experience is employed as the major technique for the development or maintenance of routine motor habits. Such habits must first be initiated, however, and work and occupational training are the basic methods used to initiate a work routine.

For those clients who cannot initiate routines by access to work training alone, physical exercise and occupational therapy are provided for priming a work routine. Skills once learned can be enhanced by being employed functionally in remunerative work.

As various aspects of a job wax or wane, some work actions are no longer performed. A good P.A.T. program will attempt to reinforce good work habits by giving the client access to job areas that keep motor and work habits in many areas alive.

Specific Work Space for Each Worker

A worker usually has a specific work space and a station. A work space may cover a city, a block, a building, or a particular workbench. Work space is assigned to an employee so that he can attend to the work assigned and can be maximally productive. Each work space should be occupied and utilized. If a worker is absent from his work space or enters a work space not assigned him, his production potential will not be reached and the employer will not realize sufficient revenue for overhead and profit.

This concept of work space is presented during the counseling, orientation, and situational sessions. A question-and-answer method may be used. For example:

Q. How would a foreman know that you aren't doing your job?

A. He can see how much work is done. He can also know that when you are absent from you work area for any length of time your work cannot be done.

Travel

Work requires than an individual be able to detach himself from home and familiar neighborhood surroundings. Most employment requires travel between home and job and an ability to travel by one's self.

During P.A.T., functional travel ability can be developed in a client by joint efforts of P.A.T. personnel and family members. Young adults and teenagers who have not developed travel ability by the time they enter a workshop setting usually need periods of supportive counseling and an opportunity for eliminating any fears that they might have. It is stressed to the client that pressures for them to travel are not rejective.

Having a person accompany the client to and from work for awhile in the beginning, as the client becomes accustomed to the travel route, is a useful method. Because clients must often travel by public transportation, familiarizing bus drivers, railroad conductors, and taxi drivers with the client's travel problems and his travel route is another method.

In the absence of a demonstrated ability to transport himself, however, a handicapped client should then be afforded special transportation to and from his residence.

Wages and Pay

Wages and cash payment for work are an essential part of the rehabilitative process. Although they are based on the productivity of each client and, sometimes, on a piecework rate having its origin in prevailing labor costs, they represent a reward for productivity. An increase signifies approval. A decrease in wages or cash payments is adverse and shows disapprobation of decreased productivity.

Feelings toward wage raises and decreases can be utilized to reach the objectives of individual and group counseling and group discussions.

Safety

A worker must avoid injury to himself and others. All workers are expected to anticipate danger and to avoid hazards. For a person to be employable, he must have an intrinsic capacity to comprehend safety concepts and to employ ample caution in the performance of different jobs.

During P.A.T., each client's concept of safety needs to be assessed in order to prevent accidents and to aid each client to understand the day-to-day hazards of a work environment. Safety habits must be explained carefully. If a conception of safety habits is lacking, work experience, individual and group counseling, and situational explanations are used to aid the client's developmental comprehension of safety in his work frame-of-mind. On a job, appropriate clothes for health and safety must be worn. Where aprons, uniforms, and other cloth items are needed for work, the reasons must be explained and the client must indicate an understanding of the necessity for such safety demands. A check must be made to see if the client has grasped safety concepts. Short sleeve shirts and no ties are essential requirements for persons working near machinery; hair nets worn by women are necessary for industrial safety.

Smoking Habits

Smoking in appropriate places, which are usually well-defined, is permissible in many industries. Since there are many fire hazards in industry, especially in production work, violation of even minor smoking regulations may often result in dismissal. Thus, even if smoking itself is permissible, knowing when and where to do so becomes a factor in maintaining the job. Frequent "smoke breaks" detract from an individual's productivity. Haphazard disposal of ashes and butts can dirty the work area as well as the goods. Smoking in food preparation areas is both a safety and a health hazard. Therefore, early development of acceptable smoking habits is vital to a client's success on the job.

Orientation and group discussion sessions present excellent opportunities for determining smoking habits. Role playing can enhance an individual's understanding of employer attitudes. It can demonstrate effectively what may happen if a person dsplays poor smokng habits. For example, in the investigator's experience, a client was working in a factory where machine parts were cleaned regularly with gasoline. One day he lit a cigarette. The workers immediately rushed out of the area where the gasoline was being used. His poor judgment resulted in his being immediately dismissed.

Smoking and safety habits fall into the area of imperatives. When such habits are dangerous, intensive situational education, counseling, and action is necessary so that the client need not be denied access to the workshop while minimal safety habits are established.

Jobs Available to the Multihandicapped

Most jobs available to the multihandicapped could be termed "peripheral" jobs. In a production setting, a retarded individual is most often used in porter work, packing, loading trucks, and service-type work rather than in the production end of the business. If the multihandicapped worker is given an opportunity to work in production and assembly, it is most often on a job that is quite routine, with minimal sequences of changes. Many successful placements of such clients have been in service industries and food service. They have also been successful in hospital pantry work and cleaning services (floor waxing, dusting, furniture polishing, etc.).

Once trained in an action, a client may be very meticulous in the performance of that action. Though output may not be great, quality can be good.

Some people working in the service industries and food service field are migratory and transient. The status of these workers is, in the United States, not very high. Pay is low. Since these jobs are mainly unskilled, available labor usually is in large supply. As a result, authority demands are often more stringent, violations are dealt with severely, and the working atmosphere is sometimes more abusive than in that of higher status jobs. Consequently, the handicapped person must be conditioned to adapt to an environment which may be unpleasant and apparently rejective. This is doubly hard for the handicapped, who have already experienced a good deal of rejection. However, an attempt is made to instruct employers of the handicapped. An emphasis is placed on the positive nature of the problem, as it is a fact that such individuals can perform satisfactory work, even though output may be in the medium range.

Employment affords the multihandicapped person greater independence and recognition than he would receive as a more dependent individual. For example, the client who formerly wandered about his community aimlessly, with nothing to do, got a job as a building superintendent's assistant. He was able to dress better, become a paying customer at neighborhood stores, and, eventually, was more acceptable to other youths in the community. This new-found acceptance afforded him the opportunity for dates and inclusion in sports and games. He was also able to contribute financially at home.

Work Interruptions

Certain basic interruptions are accepted in job situations. These may be regular breaks, trips to the washroom, occasionally arriving late or leaving early, etc. Frequent and lengthy interruptions, however, have an adverse affect on job success. Repeated tardiness after breaks, too many trips to the washroom, and extended trips to other work areas decrease the productivity of the client. They are also cues to the employer that the client is not attending to his job properly.

The work environment and experience in a training program, therefore, must make explicit demands from the very outset on the client, so that his experience engenders basic and acceptable work habits. Foremen and work supervisors, acting in "authority" roles, have excellent opportunities to inculcate good habits. They are in close contact with the client and can more effectively relate to the client's feelings with respect to his work habits. They have an excellent chance to enhance the client's ability to meet the demands of a real work situation.

Work Attitudes

An employee should have basic attitudes toward work that enhance both his productivity and his usefulness as a worker. Among these attitudes is a desire to maintain adequate standards of speed and accuracy. When a particular job has been completed and a new assignment is not ready, a worker can do other jobs as necessary, such as cleaning up his work space, putting minor things in order, etc. Or, he can request more work.

Industrial and service work usually require that a person do work assigned by a foreman or work supervisor. Resistance to work or destruction of work materials is not tolerated. Impatience with work not liked often causes mistakes and affects the ultimate production and value of the employee. An employer, observing evasion of or withdrawal from work or an employee refusing to do available work, often feels justified in considering dismissal of the employee. Any employer expects a worker to show job responsibility.

An employer also expects a worker to concentrate on his tasks amid distractions and to tolerate physical conditions which may be considered somewhat unpleasant but which are part of a job. If working conditions are within the limits of safety, the worker is expected to work safely.

A training program attempts to develop concepts of work tolerance. By counseling the client and enhancing proper vocational choice, resistance to work can often be overcome. The use of pay rewards and recognition can help acceptance of work not liked. The amount of pay for a given pay period can be used to measure productivity and to demonstrate to the client exactly what rewards can be derived from working, regardless of where, when, what, and how work is performed. These rewards can be used as recognition of job steadiness, job completion, and job regularity over a considerable period of time.

Another method used to develop work satisfaction is the assignment of quasi-supervisory roles to those who are able to assume them and who will benefit from such an assignment.

Concepts the Client Must Understand

A P.A.T. program attempts to make the client understand certain concepts. These are:

1. Work sets limits on activity. On a job, a work space is designated and the client must abide by this assignment.
2. Work requires attention to many things. These are specified by the employer. A worker has the power of suggestion, not designation, relative to work.

3. Production workers see very little of an item in the overall process of moving the item through production from start to finish. A worker must be able to handle items that are only partly complete without having a feeling of inadequacy or loss caused by not seeing the completion of the item. In this sense, a worker may not see an item either started or finished. His job may be to process materials without regard to their stage in production.

4. Work may become monotonous but the prospect of rewards and satisfactions can often overcome monotony. On the other hand, the result of being affected adversely by dull routine could be job loss.

Personal Habits Related to Work Adjustment

A P.A.T. Program must see to it that the client maintains good grooming habits, good health habits, and good eating habits (eating breakfast, having a proper lunch, etc.). These are all factors related to job adjustment. Classes, group discussions, and group counseling are techniques used to effect an improved self-image. Individual counseling can help solve problems that are hindering adjustment.

Positive Disapprobation (Punishment)

In the world of work, there are only two actions which may be taken for failure to meet requirements:

1. Admonishment and/or criticism.
2. Dismissal.

These are the only forms of positive disapprobation (punishment) available to a staff member in a P.A.T. program. Job loss can never be taken lightly as it generally causes removal from the program. Such an experience may lose the client participation in the program and, possibly, to any field of ultimate achievement.

CHAPTER FOUR

Personal and Interpersonal Factors
And Concepts Related To Work

The behavior of one human being, whether motor of ideational, when related in any way to another human being, is interpersonal behavior. Work, therefore, may be considered a social act, involving interaction between persons on both a direct and indirect basis.

Working with Others and Dealing with People

There are very few jobs in modern industry where a single individual converts raw material into a finished product. Most individuals work with others in one way or another. Workers handle materials, process them, and pass them on to others. Work often requires that two individuals perform the same task as helpers, teamworkers, or mutual assistants.

This aspect of work gives rise to the basic interpersonal relationships that exist on a job. It underscores the necessity for all workers to conform to some basic standard of behavior that will be accepted by all persons involved.

Ability to Face Impersonal Relations and to be Impersonal

A person leaving the home environment for a job comes into contact with large numbers of people with whom he is unacquainted. As many handicapped individuals have experienced long periods of dependency, they often exhibit a great need for making contact with people. They may have to ask for directions or help in doing things—things they would not need to do after finishing a P.A.T. program.

The client, in his contact with others, not only has a need to be instructed but also a social need. On a job, however, production is important. If a person becomes involved in talking with others and not sticking to the assigned task, or if he leaves his own place of work too often, his work will suffer.

The client will also experience the fact that others will come and go from the work area without any effect on persons already in that area. He must learn to face such impersonal relations. In short, he must learn how to be independent in an environment which, at times, may be impersonal.

The ability to face this situation is a factor in a person's adjustment to work. Methods used to develop such an ability are authority-discipline roles on the part of supervisors or foremen, role playing, individual and group counseling, peer influences, and discussion groups.

Ability to Meet and Deal with the Public

Many jobs necessitate interpersonal relations with brief acquaintances, customers, and persons not directly related to a job or work situation. Ability to meet and deal with the public on an impersonal basis is an important aspect of work. One should be polite and well-groomed, able to communicate verbally, and generally have acceptable manners and behavior.

The *method triad* is used by P.A.T.: evaluating the problem, assessing the problem, and developing a training plan for effecting a client's ability to function properly. Specific techniques used may be counseling, role playing, and work experience itself.

Competition (Comparison with Other Workers)

The essential nature of a job is that a worker performs assigned tasks well and functions up to the limits of the job's demands satisfactorily. Workers may be compared to each other with respect to their performance. One worker may emerge from such a comparison as more (or less) desirable an employee than another worker. Thus, in a sense, workers compete not only for the job itself but also to keep it.

Handicapped individuals may be placed in such a competitive situation. If they can face competition by working optimally, they can often hold their own and, in many instances, can keep their jobs by a good performance. The handicapped worker must work to his maximum ability to compete with the average person in even the simplest of jobs.

P.A.T. attempts to develop a client to his fullest postential and to enable him to understand that competiton, through comparison with others, is part of the world of work. Work experience, pay incentives, and approval (and praise) of work well done all help to foster this attitude and understanding on the client's part.

Reaction to Authority

Handling Authority

Handicapped workers most frequently obtain jobs with minimal status and responsibility. Consequently, many levels of authority exist above them. Survival on a job may depend on the person's ability to take orders, commands, suggestions, and supervision. Ability to withstand such pressures can be developed in the workshop by the introduction of work situation orders, and it can be ripened and hardened by selectively demanding increasing adherence to job norms. Refusal to follow proper instructions on a real job can, after all, result in dismissal.

This investigator has noted that many handicapped individuals who successfully performed in a real work situation on a *functional* level, nevertheless lost jobs because of their inability to cope with authority encountered in the real world outside.

In P.A.T., a realistic attitude toward authority is developed through manipulation of the environment and introduction of authority. Counseling is used if an adverse reaction to authority develops. Immediate handling of an adverse reation is done by the workshop foreman or supervisor. Situational (on-the-spot) counseling is employed to elicit the client's feelings and to help him handle these feelings in a more appropriate manner.

Repeated exposure to certain authority situations may develop tolerance on the part of a client to such situations. The client will then be able to behave appropriately. If an individual cannot develop appropriate behavior with respect to authority in some work situations, he may be able to cope in a different situation, either selected or sheltered.

Facing Employers and Dependence on Authority

Many handicapped individuals are overly dependent on authority for direction and cannot function on their own. They are not capable of self-direction. However, an employer cannot spend an undue amount of time in overseeing each operation. While an employer wants an employee to take supervision, he also wants him to be able to function without supervision. In other words, occasional, not continuous, supervision is the situation on many jobs.

In P.A.T., after initial instruction and careful supervision, the "presence" of authority is gradually withdrawn to a discrete distance while the client's ability to function independently is assessed. During classes, instruction, and group discussion, the relationships between authority, supervision, and independent work are presented.

Reactions are handled situationally, and more complex problems are given to counseling techniques.

Rejection by Authority

Production supervisors, because of the pressure of work, are often impersonal in given situations. This impersonality of the supervisor should not be interpreted by the client as rejection of him by the authority. Profanity and yelling at a worker, though objectionable, are entirely normal elements to be encountered in almost any job environment and do not necessarily mean rejection by authority. In the course of work, such occurrences do happen, especially in the "peripheral" work situations where many handicapped must work because of limitations.

Many handicapped persons tend to exaggerate minor social slights because they have had no former criterion of experience upon which to evaluate the actual degree of these "slights." Work hardening and work experience are the best methods of effecting adjustment to authority. Counseling, group counseling and discussions, and role playing can be used to reflect client feelings and to educate the individual toward an acceptance of authority. If a client finds it difficult to adjust to an environment which has some objectionable features, his access to employment is limited to selective or sheltered employment.

Developing Work Ability in the Handicapped

The development of handicapped individual's ability to be capable of useful work is dependent upon his ability to face the demands that work will place upon him. Such a facility to work usefully usually develops away from home. The home environments of the retarded tend to be overprotective or rejective. Away from home, an individual comes in contact with other individuals. This produces an interaction of personalities. By participating in a work setting, the client develops a sense of belonging. He begins to understand the thoughts of other people and to comprehend the perspective of another person's point of view. Thus, he begins to identify with co-workers and with work authority.

As these identifications begin to emerge, the client tries to keep pace with other workers and to develop work habits and skills often based on these identifications. In the process of work, he comes into contact with other people physically, socially, and emotionally.

The workshop fosters the development of skills in handling interpersonal relationships by offering each client an opportunity to experience new things, as well as to learn by trial and error. Production increase is recognized outwardly by pay increases and approbation and is self-recognized by the development of feelings of achievement. As the client advances in skills and productivity, recognition by others may follow. This gives the individual a feeling of self-sufficiency and independence.

In a P.A.T. setting, there are also opportunities for regression. Regression, returning to a lesser degree of development and a lower level of accomplishment, can be used in P.A.T. By going backward, the client finds himself on more solid ground emotionally and physically. This foundation can be stabilized and a more solid building of attitudes and physical abilities can begin. This process may be likened to "going back to scratch and starting all over again." This time, however, the building of an ability to cope with situations is careful and not haphazard.

Positive assets and negative factors, as they affect work adjustment, may be made more apparent as the client, by being himself, regresses and redevelops. This side of the development of a training plan is as important as any other. Regression is not to be considered failure. Rather, it is a second chance to be used toward better development. Careful handling of the situation may engender a degree of insight in the client, so that he may begin to start trying to solve his own problems rather than always relying on others to do so.

To strengthen the ability of a client to function under work and authority pressures, an opportunity for ego satisfaction should be afforded. Affection, recognition, and prestige are needed to develop client satisfaction in the face of the delayed reward system of work (pay only on paydays, etc.) and in the face of the negative pressures and demands that work places upon the individual. Psychological support of the client creates as atmosphere in which work pressure can be exerted.

Additionally, differences in learning capacities are evidenced by differences in functional achievement. During P.A.T., an attempt is made to show the client that there are, indeed, differences in ability. Some may be more capable in one area than he, others less. In a work situation, workers do different jobs and receive different wages. Again, some may receive more pay than he, some less. Whatever the differences are, they are part of a work situation; and the client is helped to see this and not to let it upset him.

Client reactions to praise, monotony, success, and failure can be evoked in a life setting. Counseling and situational handling may then lead to a better chance for adjustment to a real life situation. Ego can be strengthened through realistic success. An immature dependence on commendation for satisfaction can be reduced.

Satisfactions

Satisfaction from all levels of achievement engenders an atmosphere of motivation. It is an objective set for each client to exercise the need to help others. Some clients need an opportunity to exercise mastery. A workshop can provide such an opportunity in a constructive manner by placing a client in a situation where he can work faster or better than the others in the group.

Religions, Race, and Culture: Contact and Ethnic Difference

Religious, class, race, ethnic, cultural, social, and economic differences affect the client's attitude toward certain jobs. A client who can function as a good porter may be unable to take such a job because there is no place in the aspirations of the group he comes from for being a porter. Such work may be considered demeaning.

In some instances, working in settings with members of other ethnic or racial groups can cause clients to leave jobs. Or, they may enconter animosities based upon prejudice. A client may be able to work with a co-worker who is a member of another ethnic group. However, he may consider working under a supervisor of that ethnic group, which he considers inferior to his own, as unacceptable. One client, for example, refused to work in a hospital pantry because most of the pantry jobs were held by black workers.

If the client is in close proximity to clients of other ethnic, social, racial, or class groups, it is possible to observe both his attitude and theirs and to assess whether they can function in such surroundings. Through environmental manipulation, the client may come into contact with members of different groups in various status situations (supervisor, supervisee). The client's feelings are reflected during individual and group counseling sessions. Adverse reactions are handled situationally.

The objective of this procedure is to enable the client to function in any work situation and in any role relationship, and in settings where persons of other classes, religions, races, cultures, and ethnic groups intersect as workers and supervisors. A lack of an adjusting attitude toward differences among groups limits the client's potential employability.

The Way Others View the Client

In spite of a worker's having productive adequacy and skills, job success often depends upon the way others view a worker and the way he believes others view him. Identification (putting one's self into another's point of view) is often dependent upon a person's ability to obtain responses from others. The way one interacts with others often determines the reaction of others toward oneself.

Should an individual desire to pit his strength against another, or express a desire to injure others, he can expect to receive counter-expressions of hostility and aggresion from others. Expressing envy or jealousy is likely to bring the client reactions of hostility and animosity. If a worker uses obscene language when relating to others he will affect adversely his desirability as an employee.

Fighting, teasing, running away, rages, physical attacks, periods of non-cooperation, selfishness, stealing, disobedience, cruelty, defiance, lying, and stubbornness are all unacceptable behaviors in a real life work situation. In some cases, they may prompt dismissal.

During P.A.T., a client is often confronted with the attitudes of members of the *nonprofessional* staff. They are less likely to tolerate deviations from the norm.

An attempt is made to develop within the client a sense of responsibility for his acts. Expressions of inadequacy and inferiority are reflected in counseling. Support of a client is given by successful work experience, work simple enough so that he will be successful at it and gain satisfaction leading to a better self-image. Individual behaviors are isolated by environmental manipulation—placing the client in different situations. These behaviors may then be assessed and corrected, if necessary. For example, observing and analyzing an individual's reaction to an angry foreman.

The general philosophy of approach is to expose the client to many different situations which might arise in the real life world of work. The client's reactions can then be observed and assessed. When reactions impair either work function or acceptability of the client by others, attempts are made to change the behavior pattern of the client to the point where he can be accepted. If this is truly not possible, the client is taught to function at the highest possible level in a selected or sheltered situation.

A client's attitudes can be observed in behaviors such as: overpoliteness; persistent fault-finding; thrusting of one's own ideas on others; demands for undue attention from fellow workers and supervisors; frequent indiscriminate complaining; crying without cause; escape into illness; and being unduly directed by others, easily discouraged, or unreliable.

All these behaviors are signs of disturbance relative to the client's attitudes on interpersonal behavior. They must be assessed and handled during more extensive counseling sessions. These behaviors are symptomatic of other underlying causes, many of which cannot be elicited by environmental manipulation. However, the client can still continue with the rest of his training in P.A.T. while these problems are being handled.

Acceptance of a Client on a Job

A client, to be considered a successful worker on a job, is expected to have the ability to act in moderation in all situations. He must make some decisions on his own. He must also restrict his social contact during work to those persons he must interact with on a specific job and within a specific work space. A client must restrict his recreational activities (playing ball, cards, etc.) to appropriate moments during the workday (lunchtime, breaks, after working hours, etc.).

The client also must be able to make legitimate requests for help but not be so helpless as to be persistently in need of aid. In addition, a worker must demonstrate an ability to shift personal desires from ideal jobs to available jobs. A worker, in summary, must be able to exhibit those basic behaviors necessary for maintenance on a job.

Meeting the Client's Needs

Once a client can demonstrate acceptable behavior on a job, his own needs, such as a more comfortable chair or an increase in pay, can be considered by an employer.

Counseling sessions during P.A.T. explore what the client wants to be in relation to what he can be. Role relationships can be explored in terms of status dynamics and the tasks through which status can be attained.

Special Problems

Special problem areas such as heterosexual relationships, homosexuality, mate selection, and masturbation, especially as they may affect work adjustment, can be handled during personal counseling. In connection with the client's living situation, parental attitudes, etc., casework may also be necessary.

Persistence of a Problem

Maladaptive behavior often may not be noted during short periods of observation. This usually shows up over a longer span of observation. A client may arrive late occasionally, become angry at other clients and supervisors, take long trips to the bathroom, or daydream excessively. Such behavior may wax and wane. An emotionally involved client, however, seems to persist in these behaviors longer than others.

For example, a client may consistently want to sit alone at his workbench, may isolate himself from others while eating, and may engage in conversation only on rare occasions with other clients. Such behavior may have a wide variety of patterns. A client may *need* to place materials in a particular sequence or pattern on his workbench. Another may continually "act up" with even the friendliest foreman. Such a client may be impelled by internal anxieties and pressures to behave in such a manner.

Competent personnel must be able to assess the problem, treat and modify the client's behavior,or refer him for special help. The professional must also be able to differentiate between compulsive behavior and overemphatic, logical procedures. Whether the action may involve floor waxing, food preparation, painting, etc., the client may be trying very hard to do something the right way. Rather than being compulsive, he is repeating learned, correct actions carefully.

The "Detached" Client

Some clients are unable to maintain contact with people and surroundings. This may be evidenced by continual day-dreaming, ritualistic mannerisms, and autistic behavior. He may fail to reply to appropriate environmental stimuli, such as being talked to, and he may fail to appreciate obvious dangers. In short, the client may be oblivious to his surroundings.

In such a case, an attempt must be made to solve the underlying problem which is causing such behavior. Environmental supportive manipulation may be used to provide a group setting. Here, work or other activities will be going on around such a client. These activities and individuals near the client will not place any demands upon him. In such close proximity, the client cannot help but sense them. Sooner or later, he will react in some way to them!

A positive reaction should be reinforced by simple commendation: "Good." "That was good." This can be followed by some sort of reward, sometimes with respect to pay. If the client acts negatively, he must be prevented from hurting himself or others, or damaging materials. Yet he will still be continued in that environment. This affords him another chance to react positively. His reactions are noted carefully.

At the Institutes, a client with acting-up behavior may be removed from the work setting until the behavior is mediated. Individual counseling and behavior modificaton are integral to dealing with such behavior, as well as maintaining the client on routine work programs once the acting-up behavior has been ameliorated.

Other Maladaptive Behavior

Other persistent, ostensible maladaptive behavior may be inappropriate rages, one-sided anger (anger not visibly provoked), sex practices in inappropriate settings (kissing in a work area, etc.), an extreme lack of a sense of modesty and privacy, and abnormal fears and suspicions.

Rage and anger must be adversively conditioned and handled in such a manner as to prevent injury to the client or others. The client is gradually brought into contact with others as he demonstrates an increasing ability to handle emotionally charged situations.

At times, clients may kiss and hold hands during breaks and at lunchtime. Two approaches to cope with such behavior and similar behavior patterns are possible:

1. A sharp, authoritarian stand to stamp out such activities as immoral and dangerous;

OR

2. A development of the client's internal controls. Eventually, he will learn to conduct himself properly without supervision.

Experience has shown that an iron-handed attitude often makes clients withdraw. They withhold their confidence and find solutions elsewhere — solutions which are often inadequate. Many clients have never been permitted to associate with members of the opposite sex unless they were under strict observation. These clients were never given the opportunity to develop proper behavior with the opposite sex.

It is a common error to believe that a handicap is accompanied by minimal sex urges, sex needs, and sexual understanding. But needs will arise and they must be handled intelligently to assist the client in dealing with such problems at his or her own level. Caution must be exercised so that problems which already exist are faced but that no new problems are accidently introduced during the process.

An occurrence of individual behavior in the shop may be made the basis for individual group counseling sessions. Guidance, behavior modification, and counseling can be used situationally to handle some individual problems. Some questions cannot be answered generally without being vague to some clients, or raising new problems in other clients.

The handicapped can develop a sense of responsibility. How much responsiblity a client can take upon himself is determined individually, and situations are constructed in which the client can exercise responsibility.

Another technique for developing appropriate behavior towards members of the opposite sex is group recreation.

CHAPTER FIVE

Competencies and Techniques Needed
By Members of a P.A.T. Staff

Personnel administering P.A.T. programs occupy key positions in the life potential of handicapped youth and adults. P.A.T. personnel may be the only trained persons who observe a client's behavior in a functional setting. Their skills, knowledge, and ability to detect problems and to handle these problems directly, or to refer a client for competent help, may be decisive in the ultimate resolution of the client's problems.

Indications that a client needs special assistance are not always clear. It is easiest to discover problems in the acting-up clients, i.e., those who express problems openly through their behavior. These acts are so obvious they cannot be ignored: destroying material, striking other workers or foremen, persistent fault-finding, flying into rages, etc. The resolution of such problems may depend upon whether or not P.A.T. personnal know what to do.

Many deep-seated problems, however, may not be acted out. They may be noted by observation only over a period of time. Withdrawal from the group, inability to make friends, detachment and a lack of awareness may be signs of deep-seated problems which are not immediately recognizable. Sudden rages exhibit a problem which must be dealt with immediately. But a problem which manifests itself passively may be just as serious, but may be overlooked. It is equally essential that this latter problem be handled correctly.

The Need for Special Competencies in P.A.T. Personnel

Personnel who engage in the treatment of the special and varying problems encountered in P.A.T. programs must have knowledge of a wide range of skills and techniques. A study by this author in 1946 showed that two-thirds of the professionals in the 37 workshops replying to a questionnaire had at least a master's degree or equivalent education. The fields most represented in this survey were psychology, education, social work, and rehabilitation counseling.

A P.A.T. program offers to each client a broad-based yet intense and individualized experience. He or she gains work experience, new and/or increased work skills, exposure to and opportunity to adapt to the realities of the work world. At the same time, the client is treated for any physical problems stemming from his disabilities through tailored physical education and therapy programs. Counseling is offered at regular as well as situational times, and the family is encouraged to take part in the client's growth and development through family casework. Finally, recreation is available that is both therapeutic and fun. Social skills are enhanced and the experience is often a strong motivating factor in increasing client productivity and social abilities.

It is not surprising, therefore, that a program entailing so many factors would require a high degree of experience, commitment and training of its staff, both professional and nonprofessional. A P.A.T. professional particularly should have at least a master's degree and one year's professional training and supervised experience in education, social work, physical education, vocational rehabilitation, psychology, or a similar field.

Roles and Status in a P.A.T. Setting

A "role" is the type of behavior that an individual exhibits in terms of what others expect or demand of him. A person assumes a role whenever he interacts with another. He also assumes different roles in different situations. This process of assuming roles is developmental, beginning in the family and moving to the playgroup, the school situation, and the working world.

As a person plays a role, he assumes a certain position or standing relative to others. This relative position is called "status."

The Professional

Merely be being in the workshop, the P.A.T. professional assumes various roles. It is essential that he or she understand the dynamics involved, for people will react to the professional simply because of his or her position. The professional can be a buffer between the client and the shop or the community; assume roles as friend, confidant, supporter, and listener. This gives the client an opportunity for reflection of feelings and enhances the counseling process. The professional should avoid assuming roles of a punitive or value effect nature, as this can seriously impair the client-professional relationship.

P.A.T. professionals must also be capable of the authority and responsibility needed to assign specific roles to nonprofessionals in the workshop, and train them to perform these roles adequately and effectively. Any regression, anxiety, and maladaptive behavior on the part of the client that may be evoked by role playing by the nonprofessionals can then be assessed by the professional in terms of the client's work adjustment. With proper treatment, the client will be better able to adapt and handle such difficult situations, whether in the shop or in the competitive job world.

It must be emphasized, however, that role playing to elicit client behavior must never exceed those situations which the client is actually likely to encounter in the working world. Undue strain or stress to the client is pointless and should be avoided.

The Nonprofessional

These individuals should possess many of the qualities of professional P.A.T. staff in order to help meet the client's needs. Men and women who demonstrate an ability to teach on a practical level and who show insight and sensitivity towards the retarded and emotionally disturbed make an invaluable contribution to the P.A.T. experience of each client.

The nonprofessional staff also act as buffers between the client and the community. But, at the same time, they also represent the demands of the community, since they assume the roles of authority, judge, peacekeeper, referee, and pay giver. Under the guidance and training of the professional staff paraprofessionals deal intensely and throughout the day with the reactions clients may have to the various roles just mentioned, helping the client to adapt and grow through the experience.

Individuals acting as work supervisors, instructors, and foremen with knowledge in specialized fields, because they work so closely with the client, can teach by example, whether it be a manual skill or a mode of behavior. They help preserve the professional-client relationship at the same time that they provide the client with supportive yet realistic opportunities to learn, improve, and grow.

Summary of Competencies Needed by P.A.T. Professionals

General

A P.A.T. professional must possess many skills and understand the various processes that are undergone in a workshop setting. Among the most important skills are:

1. *An understanding of criticism.* (punitive, nonpunitive, constructive, destructive, affectional); the uses of criticism; how it may be given in the interest of the client; and who may properly criticize. The dynamics of criticism as they relate to staff development and training must also be understood. A P.A.T. professional is responsible for environmental manipulation and assignment of roles. He must be careful when giving criticism to nonprofessional aides and foremen not to disrupt or diminish the contribution they must make themselves.

2. *An ability to anticipate problems.* Environmental manipulation may evoke maladaptive behavior and the P.A.T. professional must know how to handle the problems which may subsequently arise.

3. *An ability to give and take orders* and to make reasonable demands on other staff members.

4. *An ability to assign roles* and work space and routines to clients through the use of nonprofessionals.

5. *An understanding of the client's home and family situation* and the many ways in which those relationships may affect him or her in the shop. A client may react to other clients or supervisors in the same way that he reacts to his brothers and sisters or parents at home. This can be either positive or negative for the client. The professional must understand the origins of such behavior and the dynamics involved in altering it when necessary. Family casework may be necessary.

A P.A.T. professional, because both clients and staff encounter many different situations which must be used to help the client grow, should also have an understanding of the following:

1. Methods of creating an atmosphere for independence; the dynamics of goal attaining and success; the theory and practice of rewards.

2. The dynamics of behavior modification, authority testing; when to interfere; the dynamics of identification and projection; the concept of structure and the dynamics of permissiveness.

3. When and how to be restrictive and to use restrictive techniques; the dynamics of hostility and hatred; the dynamics of perverse behavior (obstinacy of point of view, malicious persecution and intimidation of weaker individuals, and exhibition of a "mean streak"); how to handle incorrigibles and when to exclude them; punishment and its significance.

4. The dynamics of blame, praise, threat, and humor; the dynamics of affection; encouragement and discouragement; the uses and effects of competition and cooperation; the dynamics of self-esteem, self-confidence, recognition, and support, as these concepts apply to both clients and staff.

Specialized

The P.A.T. professional should also have knowledge and training in the following areas:

1. Psychometric interpretation.

2. Interpretation of projective test and vocational test information.

3. Individual differences in learning capabilities.

4. Developmental psychology and the psychology of adolescence.

5. Counseling techniques.

6. Family dynamics.

7. Dynamics of the work world—types of occupations, job demands, etc.

8. The dynamics of race and culture contact.

9. Group dynamics and the psychodynamics of individuals in groups.

10. Working with other agencies and professionals on some cases, toward certain mutual objectives. When, how, and to whom referral of the client for additional services should be made.

In Conclusion

The work of both the professional and the nonprofessional in a P.A.T. program requires a broad range of skills, specialized abilities and training and, equally important, a spirit of commitment and a depth of sensitivity and understanding of the handicapped individuals they serve in a P.A.T. program. For it is the combination of all of these that will enrich the client's life, increase his or her skills and abilities, and enable each such person to find and keep a deserved and special place in the life of the community.

APPENDICES

APPENDIX A

Excerpts From Parent's Letters On Their Experiences At The Institutes

Ben

Ben was born a multihandicapped child. He is brain-injured, an epileptic, and suffers from Down's Syndrome. (He has exhibited some evidence of increased seizure activity during recent months.) At three years he could not sit up and was totally unaware of anyone or anything around him. He could not turn from his back to his stomach. Despite the fact that my husband, Ben's father, is a surgeon, we had been unable to find any help or advice regarding programming or physical stimulation for Ben.

We heard of S.A.'s Hospital Children's Clinic, a program for severely handicapped children and, after a request on our part, Ben was accepted. He was in this program approximately four years. We received a total evaluation, received some recommendations for physical and occupational *HOME* programs, and Ben was seen usually every three months. Ben sat by himself for the first time in June, 1971. During the spring of his sixth year we requested school placement and the Social Service Department of Saint Agnes—with the full cooperation of Dr. S., Pelham School System—placed Ben in the Saint Jude Program. At the time of placement Ben was totally helpless and withdrawn.

St. Jude, one of IAHD's chapters, promises to maintain a child in the program for so long as the parents are satisfied. It also promises that, barring a deteriorating medical condition, the child will not regress from where he is at the time of acceptance into the program. This provides a sense of comfort and security to the family. The family of *any* handicapped person has a tremendous responsibility for finding continuing adequate services for the person involved. Such care is always a financial burden and physically demanding for all involved, as these necessary services are not centrally located, readily available, or funded adequately in New York State.

Saint Jude's provides an all-inclusive program of physical activation and learning skills with a program truly tailored to the needs of the individual child. It was established by and is run under the direction of Dr. Jack M. Gootzeit, who has had twenty years of experience serving the multiple-handicapped. It is a program of complete body sensory stimulation and physical education. For five-and-a-half hours every day, Ben is stimulated in a way I have never seen equalled. The results are exciting. The program is further benefitted by the guidance of Dr. E. Chusid, consulting pediatrician, affiliated with the Mental Retardation Institute in Valhalla, New York. Saint Jude's is a year-round, uninterrupted program which includes a summer camp where each child receives swimming instruction. There are auxiliary services available at any time to the families, as Saint Jude's is dedicated to total family-school-community involvement, which is so necessary if these profoundly handicapped children and adults are to fulfill their full potential and become, to such an extent as is possible, contributing members of our society.

Ben has made great progress. It is imperative for his future well-being that he remain in this total program as it is offered by the Saint Jude Habilitation Institute. I have been assured again that as long as Ben is registered, he has permanent placement at Saint Jude's.

It is our feeling that Ben would regress with any interruption of his present program. We were told at the time of Ben's evaluation at Saint Agnes and the New York Hospital that Ben would never have walked or been able to sit up by himself.

Respectfully yours,

Jenny

Jenny is a severely handicapped child who entered the IAHD program November 13, 1975, Bronx, New York, after being at home for 11 years. At that time she could not sit, but could only lie on her back. She could not suck, and she had severe muscle contractions and deformities in her arms, legs, and her back and a malformed upper plate. At that time she rarely responded to people and events around her.

Since being in this program, she has shown significant progress to the point where she can sit in a wheelchair with supports; she can suck; some of her contractions have been reduced; and her general physical condition has improved. She now handles objects, responds to people, and is quite alert to events around her.

Sincerely yours,

Joseph

Joseph, born June 1971, is a profoundly handicapped child. His condition is a result of a medulablastoma, diagnosed in April 1973. His subsequent treatment at Roselle Park Memorial Institute, Buffalo, N.Y., was complicated by subdural hematomas, which caused his irreversible brain damage. He was admitted to a therapy program at St. A's Children's Unit in September 1974 and was evaluated at a two-month mental and physical level. He was rejected for further therapy in August 1975 by Dr. C. becuase he showed no improvement.

Fortunately for Joseph and his family, we was accepted at St. Jude Habilitation Institute when no other agency would even see him for an interview.

Joseph could not support his head, could not roll from back to stomach, could not sit, could not speak, and could not see.

Since being in this program, Joseph has shown significant progress. He can now support his head and sits in a chair with support. He tolerates physical contact and sometimes holds objects in his hand. Joseph has become aware of the world around him and is vocalizing in his own way. He cannot see because the message does not get to his brain.

As you must be aware I am not anxious for him to be withdrawn from a program where he has shown such sifnificant gains. I have been assured that as long as he is registered, Joseph has permanent placement at Saint Jude's. Can you feel the relief and joy for this family to find a place for a little boy who has suffered immeasurably?

Sincerely yours,

March 3, 1977

To Whom It May Concern:
The above child was seen by me today. He is profoundly handicapped as a result of a medulablastoma which was treated surgically. Treatment was complicated by subdural hematomas which caused irreversible brain damage. He is nonambulatory, blind, and is not toilet-trained.

Joseph entered a therapy program at St. A.'s Children's Unit, White Plains, New York, in September 1974 and was evaluated at a two-month mental and physical level. In August 1975 he was terminated by St. A's, as Dr. C. felt he showed no improvement. No agency other than St. Jude Habilitation Institute would interview the family or Joseph.

He has responded well to this program since his admission on September 19, 1975. He now can support his head, sit in a chair with support; tolerate physical contact and sometimes hold objects in his hand. He is more aware of his environment.

It is my impression that B.O.C.E.S. has no comparable program. Therefore, it is not advisable to remove Joseph from his current program.

Sincerely,

Betty

February 1, 1977

To: Committee on the Handicapped:
The program at F. Center is in no way equal to a public school program and is absolutely not comparable in hours or quality to what Betty gets at I.A.H.D. I

never saw her removed from her wheelchair for any activity at the Center, but is in a program and out of the wheelchair for 2-3 hours daily at I.A.H.D. (plus 2 academic hours).

I also base my opinion on the fact that my other daughter, Anne, also a resident at B.F., has today been taken to Brookdale Hospital on an emergency basis where she was admitted for treatment of malnutrition, dehydration, and bed sores,all of which her pediatrician states are due to disuse and lack of basic care.

Sincerely yours,

March 23, 1977

Betty has attended the Institutes of Applied Human Dynamics since September 1976. We have noticed a considerable change in her overall well-being. There has been a lessening of muscle contractures, her pallor has improved, her nutritional state has improved, she is definitely stronger, she can support herself better in her wheelchair, she has learned to stand with assistance, and on some occasions she has stood up without help. In addition, she is participating in programs where she is handling objects and is receiving auditory and sensory stimulation, which has effected positive changes in her perception.

Her current improved condition contrasts sharply with that which we observed before she started at I.A.H.D. when she could not straighten her legs for standing and was of a weaker constitution.

When we see our other child, Anne, who is bedridden and immobile at the same facility (B.F. Developmental Center), we see a program that is hardly fit for a human being.

John

To: *Committee on the Handicapped:*

For eight and one-half long years, I have been waiting for my son John to walk and talk. Because he was not toilet trained, could not speak or walk, no school or day program for the handicapped would take him.

At the beginning of December 1976, John began to attend the Institutes of Applied Human Dynamics—St. Mary's School. In this short time, I have noticed some remarkable changes in his condition. He has learned to walk the length of the room without holding on. He has learned to speak about fifteen words or more—and says some sentences.

Respectfully yours,

APPENDIX B

Procedures For Testing
Motor Functioning And Reflexes
(With Rose Marie Hughes)

Explanation of Terms for Motor Abilities Assessed

1. *Independent:*   A child or individual who has the ability of performing the indicated stage of motor functioning:
   Example: A child raises his head by himself or on command.

2. *Assistive:*   A child does not have the ability to perform the exercise unless he receives a minimum of help.
   Example: Child is held by the hand while walking.

3. *Passive/*
   Assistive: The child cannot perform a motor task unless the exercise is initiated by the child development worker, then the child takes over at a point to complete the exercise.
   Example: Child's torso is lifted from the ground and from that point, the child completes a sit-up exercise.

4. *Reflexive:*   Movement cannot be elicited independently or assistively. The child development worker then stimulates certain reflexes that are present (intact mechanisms) in the child to elicit movement.
   Example: Reflexive crawling: Child is placed in supine position, head and legs straight. Child's head is bent forward and down until chin is pressing into chest. Legs will flex in crawl position when this action is firmly done. Flexion occurs without the volition of the child.

5. *Passive:*   When reflexes cannot be elicited, the child development worker performs the complete exercise. The child does not actively or reflexively respond. This usually is an indication that connections and mechanisms are intact.

NOTE: A posture that is maintained for a long time leads to contracture in the shortened muscles and a tendency to fibrous ankylosis of the joints. This type of deformity and fixation can be prevented by regular therapeutic exercise through full range of motion with joint and muscle stretching.

PROCEDURE FOR USING GOOTZEIT'S MOTOR FUNCTIONING CHART

MOTOR ACTIVITY	TEST POSITION	PROCEDURE	POSITIVE REACTION
I. **Head Raising:**	(Spinal Extensors)		
Reflexive	Place child on table, flat on stomach, head reaching out over table edge, legs extended, hands held behind back.	Stabilize legs: press head down over table.	Head will raise in preparation for creeping. (If head does not raise, use passive procedure.)
Passive	Place child in supine position on table, legs extended.	To elicit reflex spinal and neck extension passively, hold both child's hands together at midline; other hand under child's head; press head up.	After constant repetition of exercise, child will begin to strengthen neck muscle and bring head up.
II. **Creeping:**	(Tonic Neck Reflex)		
	Place child prone on mat or table in creeping position.	Coax child to creep by using colorful toy or object in reaching range.	Child will begin to creep in preparation for crawling. (If child does not creep, use reflexive procedure.)
Reflexive	Place child prone on mat or table, legs extended.	Turn head slowly to one side and pull chin upward; then slowly reverse by rotating to other side and repeat.	Arms and legs will move alternately in creeping position.

MOTOR ACTIVITY	TEST POSITION	PROCEDURE	POSITIVE REACTION
III. **Sidelying:**	Place child on left side on mat, extend left leg, abduct right leg.	Place hand on child's chin and pull slowly toward right shoulder, then reverse procedure with child lying on right side.	When chin is held on stretch, right leg will abduct and come into flexion.
IV. **Crawling:** Reflexive	(Tonic Neck Flexion) Place child prone on mat in creeping position.	1. Place hands on both sides of child's head; lift child's head slightly, at same time push chin into chest with gentle steady pressure. 2. Wait for child to come to crawl position, then pull head forward using gravity for crawl movement.	1. Child will come to crawl position. 2. Child will begin to crawl. (If child does not come to crawl, use passive procedure.)
Passive	Place child prone on crawlagator.	Move child back and forth with toes touching ground; place colorful object in reaching range.	Child will begin to use head, arms, and legs in crawl.
V. **Sitting:**	Place child in sitting position at end of table.	Stabilize thighs and hold; release support of upper torso; gradually release stabilizing hold.	Child will maintain balance in sitting without assistance. (If not, use reflexive procedure.)

MOTOR ACTIVITY	TEST POSITION	PROCEDURE	POSITIVE REACTION
Reflexive	Place child supine on table or mat, knees hooklying (bent).	Holding back of child's head, bring head up, press chin to chest.	Child will rise to sitting position. If child is unable to rise, then abdominal muscles need strengthening.
Abdominal Muscle Exercise	Place child supine on table or mat, legs extended.	Holding back of child's head, bring head and chest up; press head and chest to knees.	Child's feet will raise off mat, thereby strengthening abdominals for sitting position.
VI. **Standing:**	Hold child under arms and "parachute" with feet touching flat on ground. Hyperextend knees to elicit joint action.	"Parachute" child, stabilize, then let go. Check for balance and equilibrium. Or, place child against wall to elicit walking reflex.	Child will show signs of righting.
VII. **Walking:**	Place child in standing position; extend arms; hold child at wrist (palms up).	Hold child by wrists (palm side up) and gradually pull off balance. Or, place child's arms over back of chair; slowly move chair.	Child will grasp worker's arms and begin to walk, or child will grasp chair and take a step.

PROCEDURE FOR USING REFLEX TESTING CHART   LEVEL ONE

SPINAL	TEST POSITION	TEST STIMULUS	POSITIVE REACTION	NEGATIVE REACTION
A) Flexor Withdrawal	Patient supine, head in midposition, legs extended.	Stimulate sole of foot.	Uncontrolled flexion response of stimulated leg.	Controlled maintenance of stimulated leg in extension or volitional withdrawal from irritation.
B) Extensor Thrust	Patient supine, head in midposition, one leg extended, opposite leg flexed.	Stimulate sole of foot of flexed leg.	Uncontrolled extension of stimulated leg.	Controlled maintenance of leg in flexion.
C) Crossed Extension I	Patient supine, head in midposition, one leg flexed, opposite leg extended.	Flex the extended leg.	On flexion of the extended leg, the opposite or initially flexed leg will extend.	On flexion of the extended leg, the opposite leg will remain flexed.
D) Cross Extension II	Patient supine, head in midposition, legs extended.	Stimulate the medial surface of one leg by tapping.	Opposite leg adducts, internally rotates, and foot plantar reflexes (typical scissor position).	No reaction of either leg.

NOTE: Normal positive reaction up to 2 months of age.

PROCEDURE FOR USING REFLEX TESTING CHART   LEVEL TWO

BRAIN STEM	TEST POSITION	TEST STIMULUS	POSITIVE REACTION	NEGATIVE REACTION
A) Asymmetrical Tonic Neck	Patient supine, head in midposition, arms and legs extended.	Turn head to one side.	Extension of arm and legs on face side or increase in extensor tone. Flexion of arm and leg on back of skull side or increase of flexor tone.	No reaction of limbs on either side.
B) Symmetrical Tonic Neck I	Patient in quadruped position or over testor's knee.	Ventroflex the head (bend head forward).	Arms flex or flexor tone dominates, legs extend or extensor tone dominates.	No change in tone of arms or legs.
C) Symmetrical Tonic Neck II	Patient in quadruped position or over testor's knee.	Dorsiflex the head (pull chin upward).	Arms extend or extensor tone dominates, legs flex or flexor tone dominates.	No change in tone of arms or legs.
D) Tonic Labyrinthine (Supine)	Patient supine, head in midposition, arms and legs extended.	The supine position (per se).	Extensor tone dominates when arms and legs are passively flexed.	No increase in extensor tone when arms and legs are passively flexed.

LEVEL TWO (Cont'd)

BRAIN STEM	TEST POSITION	TEST STIMULUS	POSITIVE REACTION	NEGATIVE REACTION
D) Tonic Labyrinthine (Prone)	Patient prone, head in midposition, legs extended, arms extended over head.	Prone position (per se).	Flexor tone dominates in arms, legs, and hips. To test for flexion reaction in hips, both knees are flexed simultaneously.	No increase in flexion tone. Arms, legs, or hips can be extended.
E) Associated Reactions	Patient supine	Have patient squeeze an object (with a hemiplegic, squeeze with uninvolved hand).	Mirroring of opposite limb and/or increase of tone in other parts of the body.	No reaction, or minimal reaction and increase of tone parts of the body.
F) Positive Supporting Reaction	Hold patient in standing position.	Bounce several times on soles of feet.	Increase of extensor tone in legs. Plantar flexion of feet.	No increase of tone.
G) Negative Supporting Reactions	Hold patient in standing position.	Bounce several times on soles of feet; hold patient in space.	Increase of flexor tone in legs.	No increase in flexor tone.

NOTE: Normal positive reactions from 4 to 6 months of age.

PROCEDURE FOR USING REFLEX TESTING CHART   LEVEL THREE

MIDBRAIN	TEST POSITION	TEST STIMULUS	POSITIVE REACTION	NEGATIVE REACTION
A) Neck Righting	Patient supine, head in midposition, arms and legs extended.	Rotate head to one side, assistively or passively.	Body rotates as a whole in the same direction as the head.	Body will not rotate.
B) Body Righting (Acting on the body)	Patient supine, haed in midposition, arms and legs extended.	Rotate head to one side.	Segmental rotation of trunk between shoulders and below head turns; then shoulders; finally pelvis.	Body rotates as a whole (neck righting) and not segmentally.

NOTE: Above normal positive reactions emerge about 6 months of age.

C) Labyrinthine Righting (Acting on the Head I)	Hold blindfolded patient in space, prone position.	Prone position in space.	Head raises to normal position, face vertical.	Head does not raise automatically to the normal position.

NOTE: Normal positive reaction emerges about 2 months and continues through life.

Labyrinthine Righting (Acting on the Head II)	Hold blindfolded patient in space, supine position.	Supine position in space.	Head raises to normal position, face vertical, mouth horizontal.	Head does not raise automatically to the normal position.

NOTE: Normal positive reaction about 6 months and continues throughout life.

LEVEL THREE (Cont'd)

MIDBRAIN	TEST POSITION	TEST STIMULUS	POSITIVE REACTION	NEGATIVE REACTION
Labyrinthine Righting (Acting on the Head III)	Hold blindfolded patient in space, hold around pelvis.	Tilt to the right.	Head rights itself to normal position, face vertical, mouth horizontal.	Head does not right itself automatically to the normal position.
Labyrinthine Righting (Acting on the Head IV)	Hold blindfolded patient in space, hold around pelvis.	Tilt to the left.	Head rights itself to normal position, face vertical.	Head does not right itself automatically to the normal position.

NOTE: Normal positive reaction 6 to 8 months and throughout life.

D) Optical Righting I	Hold patient in space, prone.	Prone position in space (per se).	Head rights itself to normal position, face vertical.	Head does not raise automatically.

NOTE: Normal positive reaction 1 to 2 months of age.

Optical Righting II	Hold patient in space, supine position.	Supine position in space (per se).	Head raises to normal position, face vertical, mouth horizontal.	Head does not raise automatically to normal position.
Optical Righting III; IV	Hold patient in space, hold around pelvis.	III — Tilt to right. IV — Tilt to left.	Head rights itself to normal position, face vertical.	Head does not right itself automatically.

NOTE: Normal positive reaction 6 to 8 months of age.

LEVEL THREE (Cont'd)

MIDBRAIN	TEST POSITION	TEST STIMULUS	POSITIVE REACTION	NEGATIVE REACTION
E) Amphibian Reaction	Patient prone, head in midposition, legs extended, arms extended over head.	Lift pelvis on one side.	Automatic flexion of arm, hip, and knee on same side.	Flexion of arm, hip, and knee cannot be elicited.

NOTE: Normal positive reaction 6 months of age throughout life.

PROCEDURE FOR USING REFLEX TESTING CHART   LEVEL FOUR

CORTICAL (Equilib.)	TEST POSITION	TEST STIMULUS	POSITIVE REACTION	NEGATIVE REACTION
A) Prone-Lying	Patient prone on tilt board, arms and legs extended.	Tilt board to one side.	Righting of head and thorax, abduction and extension of arm and leg on raise side (equilibrium reaction); protective reaction on lower side of board.	Head and thorax do not right themselves, no equilibrium or protective reactions.

NOTE: Normal positive reaction—6 months on.

B) Supine-Lying	Patient supine on tilt board.	Tilt board to one side.	Righting of head, abduction, and extension of arm and leg on raised side (equilibrium reaction); protective reaction on lowered side of board.	Head and thorax do not right themselves, no equilibrium or protective reactions.

NOTE: Normal positive reactions about 6 months of age through life.

LEVEL FOUR (Cont'd)

CORTICAL (Equilib.)	TEST POSITION	TEST STIMULUS	POSITIVE REACTION	NEGATIVE REACTION
C) Kneeling	Patient in quadruped position.	Tilt to one side.	Righting of head, abduction, and extension of arm and leg on raised side and protective reaction on lowered side.	Head and thorax do not right themselves; no equilibrium or protective reactions.
NOTE: Normal positive reactions — 8 months on.				
D) Sitting	Patient seated on chair.	Pull patient to one side.	Righting of head and thorax, abduction extension of arm and leg on raised side and protective reaction on lowered side.	Head and thorax do not right themselves; no equilibrium or protective reactions.
NOTE: Normal positive reactions — 10 to 12 months through life.				

APPENDIX C

Functional Categories
Of The Multihandicapped

A. Categories

In the text which follows, the multihandicapped are categorized in 15 ways. We feel that this degress of "sorting" establishes a realistic basis for derivation of a typical "Program Day." For this reason, rather small differences between one category of client and another are identified. The categories do not emphasize I.Q. as a distinguishing characteristic. However, some "probable" I.Q.'s are included as general guidelines.

Next, we have identified seven types of programs which might occur during the "Program Day" (9 A.M.-5 P.M.). For the benefit of those not working directly in the field on a day-to-day basis, we have provided some characteristic "examples" of activities which might occur as part of a given program (except in the case of "Education," which is inclusive and has within it elements of all the others).

Table 1 makes a correlation between the seven programs and the 15 categories to show what might (typically) be a "Program Day" for a given category of handicapped person.

It should not be assumed that the mix of program formula for any given category would remain rigid. On the contrary, it is our intention to demonstrate that the program mix might be varied from category to category and, in fact, from person to person on a periodic basis. The variation would depend on the analysis and best judgment of a program designer as to the needs of each person.

Note. Categories 1 through 6 apply to children through age 16. Categories 7 through 15 are concerned with persons over that age.

Category 1

This category includes extremely handicapped persons who are neurologically, orthopedically, or emotionally impaired. There is little indication of their ability to respond to the environment, nor are there are clear signs of "awareness."

The group includes those unable to raise their heads or to move arms or legs spontaneously as well as those who have not learned to stand, creep, or crawl.

Others of this group seem to be autistic and do not react to the stimuli of the environment, but may "wander." Although their movement is spontaneous, they need to be led by others.

The category also includes those who do not show spontaneous movement but who may be induced to move reflexively or with help.

At present, prognosis for the group is problematical; change in these persons can be expected in some proportion with the amount of activity input by the staff.

Category 2

These individuals show some signs of awareness and are able to follow some direction. They move their arms and legs without help. They may be able to crawl or stand. They will move a part of the body when directed to do so. Wanderers and hyperactives may be in this group. These will respond to some direction. Neurological, orthopedic, and emotional impairment is severe but not so extreme as in Category 1. Toilet training can be accomplished.

Prognosis in this group is a little better than in Category 1 but still problematical; changes can be expected in proportion to activity input by the staff.

Category 3

These individuals are capable of following instructions and vocal directions and can accomplish the minimal activities of day-to-day living if provided assistance in learning how to proceed. Some in this category will be capable of verbal communication and will have developed motor and sensory abilities to a fair extent. In the community, these children are in the classes for trainable mentally retarded. They usually test in the 35-50 I.Q. range, but some of those testing below this level are included if they function (in general) according to the description of this category.

Present prognosis is for lifetime dependency, with continuous supervision. Some may move forwad to more independence if emotional or orthopedic problems are reduced.

Category 4

These individuals are "aware" but appear to be sluggish and slow moving. They do not develop beyond minimal levels of verbal expression. Some may learn to write their names. These are usually categorized as the "moderately" retarded.

In the community, they are found in the "lower" part of classes for the educable or "upper" part of classes for the trainable retarded and are often included in special recreation programs. Their dexterity may be fair, although impaired by problems of physical coordination. Limited attention span is also characteristic.

Category 5

These are educable persons who are mildly retarded or learning disabled. They are able to learn in special education classes. They can follow directions and supervision and can achieve some level of general education at a reduced rate of learning.

Category 6

These are similar to those in Category 5 but are older (14 to 17 years of age). They are good candidates for prevocational training and elementary vocational experience. They should be candidates for community placement.

Category 7

These are similar to those in Category 1 but are older (extremely handicapped—neurologically, orthopedically, or emotionally impaired). Physical deformity may be greater than in Category 1 because of atrophy through disuse.

Prognosis for change is poor but activity is nonetheless required to prevent further degeneration and intensification of secondary pathologies related to disuse.

Category 8

These are similar to those in Category 2 but are older (individuals who show some signs of awareness). Many are semiambulatory with severe joint distortions and contractions. The autistic and wanderers continue to wander but may respond to some vocal direction. The hyperactives will sit and will follow verbal direction from time to time.

Prognosis is for lifetime dependency; the program should be directed toward maintaining whatever abilities the individual may already have and toward advancing him to the greatest extent possible.

Category 9

These are similar to those in Category 3 but are older (capable of following instruction and vocal direction, can accomplish some minimal activities of day-to-day living).

They are toilet trained and are able to dress themselves to some extent. In the community, individuals of this category might be found at occupational day centers.

Present prognosis is for lifetime dependency, with continuous supervision.

Category 10

These are similar to those in Categor 4 but are older, 17 and up (individuals who are aware, appear sluggish and slow moving, and have minimal ability for verbal expression).

Though of low verbal ability, their performance can be developed to the level required for sheltered work. Some are capable of working productively if under good supervision. Of those, some may be able to work for pay. (Probable I.Q. 50-69)

Prognosis is for some movement into the competitive community. All in this category should have prevocational training.

Category 11

These are similar to those in Category 10. Their work performance will exceed their verbal ability. They may need help with money and personal matters, but are often independent in other activities of daily living. They learn to travel locally and can carry out a day's work.

Some in this category may achieve higher levels of sheltered employment; others will only be able to accept minimal levels of competitive employment.

Category 12

Included in this category are those whose abilities are borderline for competitive work and who have fairly well developed social awareness. (Many are similar to school dropouts and illiterate individuals within the community.) The prognosis for discharge into the communty is at least fair. They will continue to require assistance in the management of their personal affairs and in the handling of money.

Category 13

Many of these persons are capable of living in the community and functioning there competitively. Age is a consideration for those in this category. The younger ones might live at a group home and work away from the residence. These will require less assistance in personal management than those in Category 12. Many will be able to manage independently.

Category 14

Those in this category are competitive and are able to work for pay in sheltered workshops. They show more social ability than the others but may need some form of guidance. (Probable I.Q. 70-75.)

Category 15

These are older members of Category 14. These persons have more competitive ability and a higher degree of social adjustment. They can more easily be absorbed into the community, may even go to college, and some can achieve a professional status.

B. A Functional Program Outline for the Multihandicapped

1. Threshhold Activities

Objectives:
To develop awareness, focus, and attention
To form human and object relationships
To induce spontaneous activity
To induce purposeful activity
To "slow down" the hyperactive so that he can function objectively
To modify random behavior
To bring to the autistic a sense of purpose

Methods:
Inducement of reflexive movements
Organization of "passive-assistance" activities
Sensory stimulation
Habituation to background stimuli
Physical conditioning
Inducement of human contact on an elementary level

Examples:

a.   An individual is unable to raise his head. He is placed prone and his head is lifted to hyperextension. (This causes every extensor muscle of the spine and torso and legs to contract reflexively.) After periods of such stimulation, head lifting may be taken over on an active basis by the patient without assistance. Similar techniques are used to induce creeping, crawling, and standing.

b.   Patient is given blocks of various sizes, weights, and textures which are placed in his hand so that he may sense their differences. Other objects which are warm, hot, cold, or icy are placed in his hands or close to his lips so that he may sense temperature.

c.   A group of children is placed in a circle. The children are induced (passive-assistively) to join hands with volunteers, attendants, and other children. The circle is then set in motion by the staff until there is an indication that the children are taking over the action on their own. Those who are wanderers or hyperactive are brought back and held in the circle until they learn the nature of the activity and have a sense of its direction and rhythm.

Staff:

Special education teachers
Adaptive physical educators
Teaching assistants
Assistants derived from the attendant staff
Volunteers

2. *Recreational Activities*

Objectives:

To develop self-control
To develop a sense of purpose in the use of physical and emotional energies
To develop interpersonal relations in group situations
To develop object relations
To develop social relations

Methods:

Group games
Sports
Swimming
Social events
Entertainments
Hobbies
Arts and crafts

Examples:

a.   A group of 10-12 are seated in a circle. One rolls a regulation volleyball to another who receives it and redirects the ball to someone else.

b.   A group sits at a low table coloring or drawing with a large box of crayons for "community use" in the center of the table.

c.   Beanbag throwing at a target provides an opportunity to wait in line, throw the beanbag, and make way for someone else.

d. Seasonal parties (New Year's Eve, etc.) provide a chance for those of varying ages with varying degrees of disability to mix with each other, with volunteers, and with staff in a social situation.

e. Painting for pleasure.

f. Modeling with clay.

Staff:
Recreationists
Assistants
Volunteers

3. Developmental Physical Activities

Objectives:
To improve coordination
To improve physical condition
To increase ability to withstand stress
To teach skills needed for "structured" physical activities
To provide therapeutic techniques for increasing the abilities of those who are neurologically or orthopedically impaired
To prevent secondary disabilities which might result from atrophy through disuse

Methods:
Exercise
Games
Sports

Examples:
a. Group calisthenics
b. Working on a stationary bicycle
c. Rack climbing
d. Volleyball and softball games
e. Games of stoop tag and forms of hopscotch and jump rope
f. Organization of wheelchair basketball games

Staff:
Special education teachers
Adaptive physical educators
Recreationists
Assistants derived from the attendant staff
Volunteers

4. Supportive Activities

Objectives:
To maintain the ability to be active
To acquire and maintain a sense of personal worth
To develop the ability to work in a group setting

Methods:
Simple productive activities

Arts and crafts
Music and dance
Activities of daily living

Examples:
"Occupational Day Center activities" such as
a. Sorting buttons
b. Banding construction paper
c. Envelope stuffing
d. Washing dishes
e. Making sandwiches
f. Gardening

Staff:
Special education teachers
Nutritionists
Recreationists
Assistants derived from attendant staff
Volunteers

5. *Education*

Objectives:
To induce the ability to use symbols in reading, writing, arithmetic
To identify and teach the tools of expression
To induce an ability for reasoning and dealing with abstractions
Preparation for everyday life in the community

Methods:
Group instruction
Individual instruction
Audiovisual instruction
Use of teaching machine both for therapy and for instruction
Activities for daily living
Arts and crafts
Music and dance

Staff:
Teachers and special education teachers
Assistant teachers
Rehabilitation counselors (those program designers who are concerned with residents under 21 years of age)
Assistants derived from the attendant staff
Volunteers

6. *Prevocational Training*

Objectives:
To develop motivation for accomplishment of work
To develop skills which are useful in the accomplishment of work
To develop experience with machinery

To develop experience in a sheltered workshop environment
To develop work experience for a return to the community

Methods:
Class instruction
Training with specific tools and techniques
Job tryouts
Training for effective interpersonal adjustments
Evaluation
Counseling

Examples:
a. Carpentry
b. Ceramics
c. Operation of lathe
d. Weaving
e. Work on floor maintenance: person might learn the use of a waxing machine and other cleaning devices together with the difference between various kinds of waxes, chemicals, etc.
f. Mailroom activity. Training in the use of Pitney-Bowes mailing machine, bundle tying machine, addressograph, etc.

Staff:
Vocational therapists
Occupational therapists
Mental health therapists
Special education teachers
Rehabilitation counselors
Assistants derived from attendant staff
Volunteers

7. *Work for Pay*

Objectives:
To develop a sense of personal worth
To develop the incentive and ability to become financially independent
To develop the ability to live on one's own; achieve semi-independence in the community
To hold down a full-time job

Methods:
Sheltered employment
On-the-job training
Part-time employment
Full-time employment
Personal adjustment training
Evaluation
Counseling

Examples:

a.   A person 17 years old or more who has succeeded in prevocational training (for example, floor-waxing) will be assisted to find odd jobs for which he will be paid at least minimal wages. At the age of 17 he will continue with a half-day at school, spending one half-day in semiproductive work.

b.   A 30-year-old person who has learned to cook in prevocational training is assigned a job at the agency a few miles away from his residence with the plan that if he makes good, a place to live will be found for him within the community, with the ultimate objective of discharge from being an agency client.

Staff:

Rehabilitation counselors
Social case workers
Vocational therapists
Assistants derived from attendant staff
Volunteers
Voluntary agency staff

The tabulation correlates 15 categories of residents with seven types of programs. The correlation represents a hypothetical point in time and would be subject to change at the discretion of the program designers.

CORRELATION: 15 CATEGORIES OF MULTIHANDICAPPED 7 PROGRAMS
THE PROGRAM DAY

Threshold	Recreation	Developmental, Physical	Supportive Activities	Education	Work Prevocational	for Pay
Category 1 Category 2 Category 7	Category 2 Category 3 Category 4 Category 8 Category 9 Category 11	Category 2 Category 3 Category 4 Category 5 Category 6 Category 8 Category 9 Category 10 Category 11* Category 12* Category 13* Category 14* Category 15*	Category 8 Category 9 Category 10*	Category 3 Category 4 Category 5 Category 6 Category 9 Category 10 Category 12 Category 13	Category 4 Category 6 Category 10* Category 12 Category 13 Category 14	Category 10* Category 11* Catetory 12 Category 13 Category 14 Category 15

*If required

BIBLIOGRAPHY

Abel, Theodore and Kinder, Elaine F. *The Subnormal Adolescent Girl*. New York: Columbia University Press, 1942.

Baer, Max F. and Roeber, Edward C. *Occupational Information*. Chicago: Science Research Associates, 1951.

Boles, Glen. *A Study of Attitudes of Parents of Cerebral Palsied Children*. New York: Columbia University Press, 1961.

Bridges, Clark D. *Job Placement of the Physically Handicapped*. New York: McGraw-Hill, 1946.

Burns, B. Delisle. "The Mechanisms of After Bursts in the Cerebral Cortex." *Journal of Physiology* 127 (1955): 427-446.

———. "The Production of After Bursts in Isolated Unanesthetized Cerebral Cortex." *Journal of Physiology* 125 (1954): 427-446.

Cajal, Santiago Ramon y. *Histologie du système nerveux de l'homme et des vertébrés*. Madrid: Consejo Superior de Investigaciones Cientificas, 1952.

Cannon, Walter B. and Rosenblueth, Arturo. *The Supersensitivity of Denervated Structures*. New York: Macmillan, 1949.

Cobb, Stanley. *Foundations of Neuropsychiatry*. Baltimore: Williams and Wilkins, 1948.

Cohen, Julius S. "A Workshop Operation Within the Framework of a State Institution." *American Journal of Mental Deficiency,* July 1961.

Delp, Harold A. "Criteria for Vocational Training of the Mentally Retarded." *The Training School Bulletin,* August 1957, p. 16.

Deny-Brown, D. "On the Nature of Postural Reflexes." *Proceedings of the Royal Society of London* (1929): 252.

DiMichael, Salvatore G., ed. *Vocational Rehabilitation of the Mentally Retarded*. Washington, D.C.: Office of Vocational Rehabilitation, Government Printing Office, 1950.

Dorland, W.A. Newman. *The American Illustrated Medical Dictionary*. Philadelphia: W.B. Saunders, 1947.

Eccles, John C. *The Neurophysiological Basis of Mind*. Oxford: Clarendon Press, 1953.

Freeman, G.L. *The Energetics of Human Behavior*. Ithaca: Cornell University Press, 1948.

———. *Physiological Psychology*. New York: Van Nostrand, 1948.

Fulton, John F. *Physiology of the Nervous System*. New York: Oxford University Press, 1951.

Gellhorn, Ernest. *Physiological Foundation of Neurology and Psychiatry*. Minneapolis: The University of Minnesota Press, 1953.

Granit, Ragnar. *Receptors and Sensory Perception*. New Haven: Yale University Press, 1955.

Grinker, Roy R. and Busy, Paul C. *Neurology*. Springfield, Illinois: Charles C. Thomas, 1951.

Haldane, J.B.S. *What Is Life?* New York: Bone and Gaer, 1947.

Hamilton, Kenneth W. *Counseling the Handicapped.* New York: The Ronald Press, 1950.

Harlow, Harry F. and Woolsey, C.N. *Biological and Biochemical Bases of Behavior.* Madison: The University of Wisconsin Press, 1958.

Hauber, V.A. *Essentials of Zoology.* New York: Appleton-Century-Crofts, 1949.

Hinde, Robert A. *Animal Behavior—A Synthesis of Ethology and Comparative Psychology.* New York: McGraw-Hill, 1970.

Hoppock, Robert. *Occupational Information.* New York: McGraw-Hill, 1957.

Hull, Clark. *A Behavior System.* New Haven: Yale University Press, 1958.

Jacobs, Abraham and Weingold, Joseph T. *The Sheltered Workshop: A Community Resource for the Mentally Retarded.* New York: 1960.

Jeffress, Lloyd. *Cerebral Mechanisms of Behavior.* New York: John Wiley and Sons, 1951.

k Katz, Bernard. "Action Potentials from Sensory Nerve Endings." *Journal of Physiology* 3 (1950): 248-260.

———. "Depolarization of Sensory Terminals and the Institution of Impulses in the Muscle Spindle." *Journal of Physiology* 2 (1950): 261-268.

Landis, Paul H. *Adolescence and Youth.* New York: McGraw-Hill, 1947.

Lythe, Howard G. "Standards for Sheltered Workshops: Development, Present Status, and Future." *Journal of Rehabilitation,* Nov.-Dec. 1961.

Mackie, Rowaine P., et al. *Preparation of Mentally Retarded Youth for Gainful Employment.* U.S. Department of Health, Education, and Welfare. Washington: Government Printing Office, 1959.

Maurer, O. Hobert. *Learning Theory and Behavior.* New York: John Wiley and Sons, 1960.

National Committee on Sheltered Workshops and Homebound Programs. *Sheltered Workshops and Homebound Programs (A Handbook).* Washington: National Committee on Sheltered Workshops and Homebound Programs, 1952.

Osgood, Charles S. *Method and Theory in Experimental Psychology.* New York: Oxford University Press, 1953.

Potts, Jane H. "Vocational Rehabilitation of the Mentally Retarded in Michigan." In *Vocational Rehabilitation of the Mentally Retarded,* edited by Salvatore G. DiMichael, pp. 147-1449. Washington, D.C.: Office of Vocational Rehabilitation, Government Printing Office, 1950.

Pavlov, I.P. *Lectures on Conditioned Reflexes.* New York: International Publishers, 1928.

Rockower, Leonard W. *A Study of Mentally Retarded Applicants for Vocational Rehabilitation in New York City.* Washington, D.C.: Office of Vocational Rehabilitation, Government Printing Office, 1950.

Schachtel, Ernest G. *Metamorphosis.* New York: Basic Books, 1959.

Schneider, Richard C. *Physiology of Muscular Activity.* Philadelphia: W.B. Saunders, 1939.

Shartle, Carol L. *Occupational Information.* Englewood Cliffs, N.J.: Prentice-Hall, 1952.

Sherington, Charles, *Man On His Nature.* New York: Doubleday Anchor Books, Doubleday & Company, 1953.

_____. *The Integrative Action of the Nervous System.* New Haven: Yale University Press, 1948.

Skinhoj, Erik; Lassen, N.A.; and Ingvar, D.H. "Brain Function and Blood Flow." *Scientific American,* October 1978, pp. 62-72.

Spitz, Rene A. *The First Year of Life.* New York: International University Press, 1965.

Strauss, Alfred A. and Lehtinen, Laura E. *Psychopathology and Education of the Brain-Injured Child.* New York: Grune & Stratton, 1948.

Tokay, Elbert. *Fundamentals of Physiology. The Human Body and How It Works.* 2nd rev. ed. New York: Barnes & Noble Books/Harper & Row, 1967.

United States Department of Labor. *The American Workers Fact Book.* Washington, D.C.: United States Government Printing Office, 1956.

Wiener, Norbert. *Cybernetics.* New York: John Wiley & Sons, 1948.

Windle, William F. *Physiology of the Fetus.* Philadelphia: W.B. Saunders, 1940.

Wortis, Joseph. *Soviet Psychiatry.* New York: Williams and Wilkins, 1950.

Young, Kimball. *Personality and Problems of Adjustment.* New York: F.S. Crofts, 1940.

INDEX

Abdominals, 64-65
Activity, 23, 33-35, 135
  and the brain, 26
Attention, 86
Attention span, 153-54
Auditory sense, 52-54
Authority, 162-64
  necessity for, 163
  rejection by, 163-64
Autism, 10
Aversive conditioning, 106, 107, 115
Awareness, 82-83

Basic orientation, 51-52
Behavior, 80-81
Behavior modification, 87-88, 94-104, 133
Blood, 25
Bone, 24-25
Boredom, 134
Brain development, 28-29
Brain waves, 46

Cells, 14
Cerebral cortex, 29, 30, 35-36
Cerebral Palsy, 9
Circulation, 14
Client needs, 168
Cognition, 79
Color discrimination, 107
Communication ability, 82
Competition, 162
Comprehension, 179
Consciousness, 46-47
Coordination, 148
Crawling, 69
Creeping, 67-68

Developmental Disabilities, 12, 17
  effects of D.D. on high level mental processes, 77-81.
  genesis of, 30, 50-51
Diagnostic methods, 127
  difficulties with, 127-28
  situational approach, 128
Directive method, 105, 108-09, 110, 114-15

Disuse, 14, 18, 30
Drive states, 90-91

Emotional disturbances, 11
Exercises for developing perceptive ability, 51-59
Exploratory behavior, 77

Failure at work, 120, 124
Fatigue, 32-33
Feedback, 42
Fixed action patterns, 89
Flexibility, 151-52
Focus, 85-86
Fun, 112
Functional ability, 8

Goals, 141
Gootzeit system, 88ff
Gustatory sense, 55-56

Habituation, 33, 40, 93-94
Haptic sense, 57
Hip flexion, 66-67
Homeostasis, 30-32
Hyperactivity, 86

Inactivity, 25
Inferiority, 124
Inhibition, 40
Innate Releasor Mechanisms, 12-15, 34, 51, 89
  agenesis of, 13, 50
  and learning, 43
  normal development of, 12-13
  stimulation of, 13, 51-59
  using IRM's, 15-16
Integration as aim of therapy, 116-17
Interaction, lack of, 114, 115
Ionic state, 24

Job readiness, 118, 119
Jobs for the handicapped, 157
Joints, 17

Learning, 43, 48, 79-80, 106
Letters 177-80.

Low status jobs, 158

Memory, 35, 44, 79
Methods, 1-2, 48-49, 80-81, 94-104,
    105, 108-09, 132
Motor ability, 48, 58
Motor functioning tests, 181-91
Motor habits, 135
Movement habits, 135
Movement, elicitation of, 39-40
Muscle, 17
Myogenic response, 26

Neck extension, 60-63
Nerves, 17, 24-49
    function of, 37-38
    growth of, 26, 27, 28, 30
Neural behavior nets, 90
Non-exclusion of clients, 22, 134
Non-service, 4-7, 10, 11, 19, 132
Non-stimulation, 17

Object relations, 106
Olfactory sense, 55

Parental attitudes, 124
P.A.T.
    ARC program, 126-27
    definition, 144
    diagnostic use of, 127
    function, 125, 139
    identification, 125
    lack of information on, 120
    methods in, 128-31, 140, 143,
        146-47, 162, 164-65, 172
    need for, 122
    objectives, 118-19, 143-44, 159-60
    orientation, 125
    rational for, 118
    relationships, 140
    scope, 147
    staff, 171, 172-75
Perception, 51
    exercises for developing, 51-59
Personal habits, 160
Physical condition, importance of, 123
Physical demands of employment, 123,
    150
Potential, determination of, 105
Prejudice, 165-66

Prenatal development, 2
Pressure-pain response, 56-7
Problems, 168-70
Problem solving, 79
Programs, 22
Proprioception, 57
Purposive behavior, 106, 108

Reactiveness, lack of, 108
Recreation,
    as developmental, 112
    as therapeutic, 113, 116
Reflex, 39
Reflexive exercise procedures, 60-76
Rehabilitation, total approach to, 116
Reinforcement, 93
Respiration, 15
Retardation, 8-9

Safety, 156-57
Satisfaction, 165
Seizure treatment, 84-85
Sensation, 42
Senses, 149
Sensory deficiencies, 149
Service for the handicapped, 19-23
Sheltered workshop, 142-43
Sleep, 47
Smoking, 157
Spatial sense, 57
Speech, 149
Staff, 20-22
Standing, 70-72
Stimuli, 31-32
Stimulus-Response patterns, 88-94

Therapeutic recreation, 112-17
Thermal sense, 56
Threatening situations as stimuli, 106,
    107, 109 110.
TOWER, 10
Training goals, 141-42
Travel, 155-56

Unlearned reflexes, 88
Use, effects of, 2, 14

Visual sense, 54
Vocational guidance, 130

Walking, 73-74
Work, 144-45
    adjustment to, 122
    as basis for individual value, 120-21
    as social, 161
    as training, 128-30
    attitudes toward, 159
    concentration necessary for, 153
    habits, 153-62
    handicapped and, 145
    interruptions, 158
    regularity in, 121, 154
    requirements for, 121-22
    results of, 158
    skills, 150
    space, 155